ROMANS

FOR NORMAL PEOPLE

A Guide to the Most Misused, Problematic
and Prooftexted Letter in the Bible

J. R. Daniel Kirk

The Bible for Normal People Book Series

THE BIBLE
for Normal People

ROMANS FOR NORMAL PEOPLE
Copyright © 2022 by The Bible for Normal People
Published by The Bible for Normal People
Perkiomenville, PA 18074
thebiblefornormalpeople.com

Library of Congress Control Number: 2022916732

ISBN: 978-1-7364686-2-3 (Print)
ISBN: 978-1-7364686-3-0 (eBook)

Cover design: Tessa McKay Stultz
Typesetting: Medlar Publishing Solutions Pvt Ltd., India

Printed in the USA

For Patrobas and Phlegon
I got next

TABLE OF CONTENTS

Romans = Including
Gentiles as/ Jews as one
Getting God as one/ faith of
Not about individual Salvation.
or Salvation. Salvation
means peace/ unity.

CHAPTER ONE

Romans from 30,000 Feet

Getting Romans Wrong: A Confession

I would like to begin by thanking all of you for coming to my personal confessional, otherwise known as this book on Romans. I expect to be fully absolved of all my sins by the time we get these preliminary remarks out of the way. So let's jump right in.

First, there was once a time when I knew exactly what Romans said, and my main concern was getting everyone else to acknowledge it as well. Not unrelated to this, I used to have strict standards of judgment about Bible translations.[1] Whenever I was trying to determine whether a Bible was worthy of my study and attention, I would turn to Romans 8:28. As a burgeoning Calvinist (actually, I preferred the term "predestinarian" or even "Paulinist" because I didn't learn this from John Calvin; I learned it from the Bible), the most important thing to me was that nobody malign the clear teaching of this verse. Specifically, it stated clearly to anyone who would listen, "God predestined!" Predestination. That was it. Basically, anyone who was capable of reading the Bible should agree with this theological point. I was quite the missionary about it. At the Christian summer camp where I worked

---

[1] And, since I've mentioned Bible translations, this is as good a time as any to tell you that the translations used throughout this book are my own.

during college, one of my co-counselors started joking about who the "believers" were—the people who believed in predestination.

Confessional Part 2: I didn't really care what the implications were—either for God or for me. I didn't care if people thought this made God some sort of moral monster (side note: a lot of people do think so). I didn't care if swimming in this stream of theology made me come across as arrogant. As a friend of mine, a fellow "believer," once said, "It's hard to be humble when you're right."

If it was biblical, it was what I wanted to cling to. If it was biblical, it was right. If it was right, then we needed to conform our ideas of God around it, not vice versa. If it made us jerks, well, that was a separate issue altogether.

Glad I got that off my chest. Don't we all feel better now?
"Bless me, Father, for I have sinned."

Well, here's the funny thing about my early dalliance with Romans: it was a colossal exercise in missing the point. How I was reading it and what my interpretation of Romans was doing to my character were nearly the opposite of what it was written to accomplish.

If I had attended more carefully, I might have seen that Romans was trying to show me a better way: a better way to read the Bible. A better way to be part of a Christian community. A better way to know if I am loving God with my heart, soul, mind, and strength.

Romans: Being the Family of God

One method for assessing the faithfulness of any particular flavor of Christianity has developed deep roots over the past two thousand years. Its fruit has been particularly abundant since the time of the Reformation some five hundred years ago. It is the conviction that true Christianity is found among the people who *think* the right things.

We delineate the boundaries of the church—who is in and who is out—based on creeds. We create thousands upon thousands of denominations based on beliefs that differ from one another—sometimes by a sliver.

And, paradoxically, those of us who are Protestants turn to books like Galatians and Romans—whose sole purpose was to establish unity among warring factions in the early church—to validate our various secessions.

"I believe in predestination, so I'm not going to listen to a preacher who doesn't truly believe in the unearned grace of God."
"I believe in justification by faith, so I'd never set foot in a Catholic church."
"The only way to be buried with Christ in baptism is believer-baptism by immersion."
"Accept one another as Christ has accepted us to the glory of God."

Wait. What did you just say? "Accept one another." That's Paul. Romans 15:7. Accept one another. Receive one another into your communities. Be like Jesus to one another.

So, you believe that "the chief end of man is to glorify God and enjoy God forever"? Then glorify God here and now by receiving each other as Christ has already done. Imitate God by naming and affirming as your siblings those who call out to God, "Abba, Father"—even as God calls them God's own children. That's Romans.

Romans is about the family of God. The family God has already created. The family with estranged members. The family God intends to reunite. The family that has its squabbles. And … the family that so bears the likeness of God that observers can look at it and know exactly who God is.

Romans is not the place to search for—let alone find!—justification that ours is the only Christian tribe that is exclusively right about everything. Nor is it the place to go to prove that every human is part of some big happy God-family. Romans resists being pulled in either of these directions. The one is far too narrow. The other is not too broad, exactly … but it attempts to embrace humanity in the wrong way.

In Romans we discover what it means that Jesus is Messiah. Because Jesus is Messiah, God has recreated God's people in and around him. And through Jesus, God is recreating humanity.

In Romans, the cosmic story of humanity's reconciliation with God is brought down to the mundane business of who you go to church with on Sunday. The nature of reality, reflecting the identity and character of God, is embodied in whom you have over for dinner and what you eat and drink together.

Everything that God has promised—the creation of a people from every nation, tribe, and tongue; a body that consists of Jews and Gentiles together; a people who are holy and faithful, glorifying God under the lordship of the Father—all of this is not pushed off to some indefinite future. It has been and is being fulfilled in the arrival of Jesus and the embodiment of his lordship here and now.

This is what Romans looks like from 30,000 feet.

- The world map being redrawn by the person of Christ.
- Peoples mixing and mingling across borders that have suddenly become porous.
- Formerly desert lands now verdant.
- Former slaves now set free.
- Squabbles examined, explained, and adjudicated.
- Family collecting for a feast.
- Everyone gathered for something greater than themselves. Reconciled to God.

Here's what makes the picture pop.

Scripture

The most important thread tying Romans together is its use of biblical references. Paul mentions in the opening verse that the gospel was "promised beforehand in the scriptures" (Romans 1:2). When Paul says something at the very beginning, it's usually a preview of coming attractions. This is the case here. Romans contains about half of the scriptural quotations and allusions that are found across the thirteen letters bearing Paul's name. For some reason, scripture is particularly important for the argument Paul is making in this letter.

When you start to dig into how Paul uses his Bible (what we would call the Old Testament or the Hebrew Bible), you soon discover that you're in for a wild ride. I know that this is supposed to be a book for normal people, but I need to give the nerds a trail to sniff out on one or two things. (Like when I was a nerd working at a Christian summer camp and I started looking up all the Old Testament citations I'd stumble across in my New Testament reading. Try it sometime. But buckle up.)

Over the past forty years or so, New Testament biblical scholars have been saying that when New Testament writers quote scripture, it looks a lot more like ancient Jewish midrash than modern academic interpretation. To put that a little differently: the New Testament writers use scripture like a sermon, telling their audiences what God wanted them to hear in their current moment, rather than like a history book, telling you what the passage meant over there and back then.

Jewish Hebrew Bible scholar James Kugel did pioneering work on early Jewish Biblical interpretation—including how Old Testament writers themselves interpreted and reinterpreted what came before. His magnum opus, *Traditions of the Bible*, chronicles the diverse ways that Jewish biblical interpretation, including the interpretations of Jews around the time of Jesus and Paul, was always an exercise in bringing the scriptures of the past to bear on the present.[2] Paul and the other New Testament writers were themselves Jews who also read the Bible this way. We might summarize the approach of early Jews (including the NT writers) like this: if scripture is where God has spoken, and if we are the people of God, then God uses scripture to speak to us about what is happening *now*.

---

[2] James L. Kugel, *Traditions of the Bible: A Guide to the Bible as It Was at the Start of the Common Era* (Cambridge, MA: Harvard University Press, 1999).

This is especially the case when a group of Jews believed that their community, or their leader, were the fulfillment of God's promises. The people who wrote the Dead Sea Scrolls included a lot of biblical interpretation. Verses that modern Christians would read as predicting Jesus as Messiah were taken by this community to refer to their founding leader, the Teacher of Righteousness. These same passages might be read by a modern biblical scholar as referring to a prophet, a king or even all of Israel returning from Assyrian or Babylonian exile.

The bottom-line, single-most-important principle of ancient biblical interpretation is this: what God has done in the present determines the meaning of what God said in the past. When Jesus's followers confessed that he was the Messiah, the only possible conclusion was that the entirety of scripture pointed to the events of Jesus's life, death and resurrection, and to the community that these events formed. Dutch New Testament scholar Herman Ridderbos observed this in his widely read book on Paul's theology.[3] And E.P. Sanders captured this pattern of thought in the phrase "from solution to plight"—i.e., what Paul thought was wrong with the world was shaped by his understanding of what God had done to solve the problem in Christ.[4]

This can be a little disconcerting for a modern reader. We like to think that the biblical writers are just giving us everything "straight." But it's not straight. It's refracted through the lens of Jesus. In Romans, Jesus's resurrection is the single most important factor influencing how Paul interprets scripture.[5] Here's the invitation: let's allow Paul to show us how he reads the Bible, rather than telling him how he has to do it according to our modern sensibilities. In my experience, we get a lot further with understanding Paul if we allow him to be a first-century

---

[3] Herman J. Ridderbos, *Paul: An Outline of His Theology* (trans. John R. de Witt; Grand Rapids: Eerdmans, 1975).

[4] E. P. Sanders, *Paul and Palestinian Judaism: A Comparison of Patterns of Religion* (London: SPCK, 1977).

[5] This idea is thoroughly explored in what may well be the most humbly named book of the early twenty-first century: J. R. Daniel Kirk's, *Unlocking Romans: Resurrection and the Justification of God* (Grand Rapids: Eerdmans, 2008).

Jewish biblical interpreter, and we don't try to make him into a modern biblical scholar. Paul's arguments and the claims he makes from scripture are not "objectively true" readings. This means that they are only as strong as his starting point. If we share Paul's starting point—Jesus is the Messiah—then we don't need to worry about "objectivity." What we have is the true story of the faithfulness of God.

The Situation (Uh-oh)

Paul wrote Romans to address a specific situation. Let me say this differently. Romans is *not* Paul's systematic theology. It's not a timeless bit of reflection on all the awesome stuff that God has done. Romans has often been read like this, especially because Paul had never been to Rome, and there's no indication he had received any specific communication about the situation on the ground.

On the one hand, the letter expresses specific concerns. But on the other hand, while those concerns may reflect what's happening in Rome, they also reflect tensions in Paul's churches on the Greek peninsula and in Asia Minor (modern-day Turkey), and Jerusalem may well be the eye of the storm. More nerd fun! Scholars debate which of these locations is the primary target for Romans' argument.[6] Has Paul heard some things—perhaps from the friends he lists in chapter 16—about the church in Rome that he's trying to smooth out? Is he looking to Jerusalem, where he is anticipating a lukewarm-at-best reception to the financial collection he's taken up from his Gentile churches for the Jewish people there (Romans 15:30–32)? Or, bonus option, is Paul really trying to make a case for why he and his message should be monetarily supported as he goes beyond Rome to Spain (Romans 15:23–24)?

---

[6] See Karl P. Donfried, ed., *The Romans Debate* (Peabody, MA: Hendrickson, 1991), for a litany of scholars advancing different ideas about how to understand Paul's purpose in writing the letter.

Reading Paul's letter well doesn't depend on landing on any one of the positions enumerated above. Here's what you do need to know: the Jews who heard the early church's message are largely uninterested in the idea that Jesus is the Messiah, so the early Jesus movement is full of Gentiles (non-Jews). Moreover, Paul is advocating vociferously for including the Gentiles without requiring them to follow Jewish law or customs (especially circumcision, Sabbath keeping—which is one of the Ten Commandments!—and food laws). So if the Jews aren't joining up to this new movement, and the Gentiles refuse to adopt the visible customs and practices central to Jewish identity, then this new movement—under Paul's leadership—is no longer distinctively Jewish. This creates at least three problems.

The first problem is God's. Slow down and take a second on this one. The fact that the Jews are not swarming to Jesus as Messiah is a problem for God. How can God be faithful if God's own people are not enjoying the benefits of God's great and final act of salvation? Paul argues that God still is just, righteous and faithful, even though the majority of the Jewish people have not entrusted themselves to Jesus as messiah.

The second problem is on the ground. What are Gentiles to make of Jews?

Pause.

We interrupt the flow of this chapter to bring you the following overview of the history of Jews in Rome and what it might have to do with Romans. The Roman historian Suetonius tells us that sometime around 50 CE the Roman Emperor Claudius expelled the Jews from Rome due to an intolerable level of conflict about "Chrestus" (compare Acts 18:2). It is often argued that this is a reference to Christ. Several years later, the Jews were allowed to return.

Romans appears to reflect a situation in which Jews, including Christian Jews, are returning to Rome. Note, for instance, that Priscilla and Aquila, who are companions of Paul during his travels around the Aegean, are greeted in Romans 16.

So imagine this: Christian Gentiles have been worshiping Israel's God and celebrating Jesus as Messiah for years, without any Jews present at all. It becomes easy to forget the Jewish roots of the faith. Then, the Jews return, including Christian Jews. And the people have to figure out how to live together in their faith communities. Or even if they should.

Why could this be problematic? Well, imagine there's a church potluck and a few dozen people won't show up if you bring your favorite green bean casserole with bacon. Do those people get to control the food? That's just one example. We'll see more as the letter unfolds.

For now, just imagine a situation in which the Gentiles need to adjust to the Jews returning to town. And they're getting this letter from Paul.

Unpause.

Where were we? Ah yes. The second problem. The problem on the ground: What are Gentiles to make of Jews? Are the Gentiles replacing the Jews? Are they the newly favored children? How should Gentiles and Jews in the same worshiping community reconcile their different ways of life? Does it matter that some people keep kosher, but others don't? Should everyone honor the great feast days of the Jewish (read: biblical) calendar? If Jews and Gentiles are both part of the people of God, then what delineates the identity of this newly formed people?

If Gentile Christians don't need to keep the law, then what actions count as faithfulness and obedience to God? THIS. This is the question. How do you know what faithfulness to God looks like if newcomers aren't required to follow scriptural commandments?

Third, and for Paul this appears to be the most personally distressing problem, what are we to make of the non-believing Jews? How do we understand their rejection of Jesus as messiah? And what is their future?

When we're reading Romans, we need to keep the question of Jewish–Gentile relations in the forefront of our minds. Or maybe I should say: if we're paying attention, we'll see that Paul is addressing it at almost every step of the way. In order to navigate this well, we need to know that Paul's audience is the Gentiles. When he says "you," unless he is using speech in character, he is talking to what he assumes are non-Jewish readers. (He says this specifically in Romans 1:5–6 and 11:13.)

These questions about the relationship between Jews and Gentiles point us to the most significant sea-change in Pauline studies in the past fifty years. A shift in posture, sometimes called "the New Perspective on Paul," has developed. In short, New Testament scholars now recognize that Paul does not think there is anything inherently wrong with Judaism. This movement has its roots in the work of Krister Stendahl, who rightly pointed out that Paul did not see his life in Judaism as one of conflicted torment with a troubled conscience.[7] Recognizing this, Stendahl argued that "justification by faith" was not the heart and soul of Paul's theology; instead, Paul deployed justification when circumstances called for arguing that Jews and Gentiles stand on equal footing before God. E. P. Sanders and James D. G. Dunn picked up on Stendahl's theory and helped change the culture of Paul studies.[8]

What does this mean for us? Getting Romans right means threading the needle of Paul's gospel. Romans is a work of navigation, balancing the promises of God to Israel with the reality that the Jewish people have largely not accepted Jesus as Messiah, while countless Gentiles have adopted this story as their own.

As we pull back from the nerd concerns, I want to give you one very big reason why this stuff matters. It matters because anti-Judaism and anti-Semitism are, in fact, rejections of Israel's God. They are anti-Christ because they stand in opposition to Jesus's own people–the people to whom Jesus came and through whom he saves–and Jesus himself.

Anti-Judiasm (based on religion) and anti-Semitism (based on ethnic and/or racial identity) are dangers that people claiming Jesus

---

[7] Krister Stendahl, "The Apostle Paul and the Introspective Conscience of the West," *HTR* 56 (1967): 199–215.
[8] E.P. Sanders, *Paul and Palestinian Judaism* (Minneapolis: Fortess Press, 1977); James D. G. Dunn, "The New Perspective on Paul," BJRL 65 (1983): 95–122.

have succumbed to on countless occasions. Its threat did not die out at the end of World War II and the defeat of Nazi Germany. American neo-Nazis chanting "blood and soil" while marching in Charlottesville, VA, in 2017 remind us that the Jewish people are in perennial danger of becoming the targets of violent scapegoating. It is all too possible for some traditional readings of Romans to provide theological fuel for this satanic fire. If Christians view Jews as people who deny the gospel of grace because they are pridefully committed to earning salvation by works, there will be little left in Christianity to stem the rising tides of anti-Semitism. This can happen if we somehow miss God's unwavering commitment to God's people, Israel. It can happen if we miss God's commitment to God's own word and promises. It can happen if we lose sight of what the faithfulness of God truly means. Reading Romans well can literally be the difference between life and death.

The Point: The Faithfulness of God

The theology that bubbles up and bursts forth at various junctures in the letter to the Romans swirls around these questions and convictions about God's commitment to Israel and the incomprehensible failure of Israel to participate in the fulfillment that has arrived in Christ. We often don't put enough stock in the fact that God's reputation, truthfulness and fidelity are all tied to commitments God has chosen to make.

God chooses to speak through scripture. So if the Messiah's advent and all the events resulting from his coming are not found to be "biblical," then God's got a big problem.

God has chosen to enter into covenant with Israel, with Abraham and Abraham's descendants, so if God does something amazing and Israel is excluded, then God's got a big problem.

Humanity was created to bear God's image: to show the whole created order what God is like. So if God's plan of salvation doesn't restore *all* of humanity, then God's got a big problem.

Jews are not entering the Jesus movement as their way of salvation. How, then, can Jesus be Messiah? How can God be faithful? What hope is there for the world? Here's how Paul tackles it.

Romans 1:1–1:18 is an introduction of sorts. It stakes out the bold claims that Paul will substantiate throughout the letter. First, scripture foresees the resurrected Jesus, who is, in himself, the embodiment of the faithfulness of God. Second, God's faithfulness through Jesus is found not only in loyalty to Israel and fulfillment of scripture, but also the inclusion of the Gentiles. Third, human faithfulness to God is reconfigured around this Jesus story.

Romans 1:19–4:25 presents a radical redefinition of the people of God. In these chapters Paul goes so far as to redefine "Jew" and "Israel" (although he will not be consistent about this throughout the letter). He transforms the meaning of these words by saying that Jewishness is about inward, heart circumcision, rather than external circumcision and physical descent from Abraham. According to Paul, a child of Abraham believes in the God who raises the dead—i.e., the God of Paul's Gospel message. He recasts the identity of the people of God, in part, by claiming that all humans, Jews and Gentiles alike, are sinful. And in the face of this universal sinfulness, Jesus's faithfulness in going to the cross, rather than Jewish faithfulness in keeping torah, leads to divine approval. Jesus is the way to God for everyone, both Jews and Gentiles. Jewishness, i.e., obeying and embodying the scriptures we refer to as the Law,[9] no longer defines the people of God.

---

[9] This one's for the nerds: Law (capital L) refers to the first five books of the Bible, a.k.a the Pentateuch, while law (lowercase l) refers to the specific laws these five books contain, a.k.a. Mosaic law or Jewish law. You'll see both used throughout this book. But please know that I did this only under dire threat from my editors. I'm not entirely sure that Paul keeps these things separate and I was rarely sure which to choose myself. So if your own thinking about "Law" bleeds over into "law" sometimes, or vice versa, you're probably doing it right.

Romans 5:1–8:39 builds on the idea of divine approval (i.e., justification) first broached in chapters 3–4. It maps out how to get from the present moment—being a sinner needing forgiveness—to the final judgment: being proclaimed a part of God's family, and therefore finally vindicated (a.k.a., "justified"). This line from cross to judgment seat is drawn through the transformative work of the Spirit. That Spirit frees people from enslavement to sin, allowing them to participate in new life. This new life that God offers people is nothing less than the resurrection life that the Spirit gave to Jesus. The flip side of this argument is that the Spirit is doing what the law was unable to do. This is why the people of God are defined by the resurrected Messiah rather than by the law.

The movement from here to final glory is the movement of Jesus's own story: suffering with him now in order to be glorified with him in the future. This is the narrative that delineates people as children of God, even as Jesus is the firstborn son of God. At the exodus, God referred to Israel as God's firstborn son. Now, Jesus takes on that role and bears the image that others will bear as well. And so the redefinition of the people of God continues. A new creation is held in the burgeoning resurrection life that God's people are experiencing. This is what divine faithfulness looks like.

Romans 9:1–11:36 is the beating heart of the book. It is the "Houston, we have a problem" moment that pulls back the curtain on why Paul makes so many arguments that feel strange or shocking, why he treats the law the way he does, why he so tightly connects Jesus with vindication in the final judgment. Here is where Paul wrestles with the incongruity, the seeming impossibility that the Jewish people would be left out of God's great saving act.

There really is a problem. Jewish people really are being left on the side. Paul appeals to divine sovereignty to explain this, and ultimately sees Jesus as the "stumbling stone" that has kept Israel on the sidelines. Paul offers some of his most creative reinterpretations of scripture to show that entrusting oneself to the resurrected Christ, not obeying

commandments, is what the law points people to. But most importantly, in Romans 11, Paul argues that God is not in fact finished with
Israel. There are some who are already part of the Jesus-following community. And Paul is convinced that his own mission to the Gentiles
will have the paradoxical effect of rebounding to Israel and leading
them to repentance and salvation. Paul's mission will be instrumental
in God fulfilling God's promises to Israel and the Jews streaming into
the family that God established with Jesus.

Romans 12:1–13:14 offers instruction on how to live as the community that God is creating and how to live as a people whose lives
narrate the death and resurrection of Jesus. Bodies offered as living
sacrifices belong to people who serve each other in humility. People
who love one another above all else, who reflect Jesus's resurrection and
the light of the new day dawning. This "fulfills the law," even if food
regulations are not kept, days are not observed, and penises are not
circumcised.

Romans 14:1–15:13 could probably be grouped with the previous
two chapters under "instructions for life together," but they have a
specific focus that I don't want to get lost. These chapters explicitly lay
out how law-keeping Jews and law-free Gentiles can live in community with each other. Once again, embodying the Jesus story becomes
paramount. Accept one another. Don't look to please yourself, but act
for the good of your neighbor—like Christ did when he died for you.

For a people (us) who spend most of our public energies fighting
for our own way and carving out reasons to act in accordance with our
own convictions and desires, Romans 14–15 is a wake-up call, reminding us that walking in the way of Jesus means laying down our lives so
that our sisters and brothers might live. Unfortunately, we as a church
spend much of our energy articulating why our boundary markers are
the correct ones, and why our standards of righteousness are inviolable.
In rebuke, Romans 14–15 teaches us that the people of God are those
whom God has accepted. Not those who conform to our theology.

Not those who conform to our practice. The Jewish people had more tradition and biblical knowledge than anyone, but they still didn't hold the trump cards. The Gentiles were acting out of faithfulness, but their opinions and practices weren't the last word, either. The last word is that God has accepted both.

Romans 15:14–16:27 puts a cap on the letter. It offers some personal greetings from church leaders and salutations to Roman Christians. It provides a bit of a window into what Paul is up against personally. He's writing to Rome, west of where he currently sits in Corinth. But his mind is on the east. In Jerusalem. Where he's going. And he's not sure how it will turn out. Paul's plan is to bring money from his Gentile churches to the Jewish believers. A token of unity, his own way of concurring with God that Jews and Gentiles are both part of one body, one family.

But things aren't looking good. Galatia was supposed to participate in the collection (1 Corinthians 16:1), but Paul doesn't mention them here in his list of participants (Romans 15:26). It seems that Paul might have lost the argument he made in Galatians. His law-free mission to the Gentiles is in jeopardy. A group in Jerusalem has come to a very different conclusion about how God might still be faithful to the Jews: they are claiming that Jesus is the doorway for converts to Judaism—as marked by keeping the law of Moses. Paul is gravely concerned (Romans 15:31). This is the clearest indication we get of the situation that has given rise to the whole letter.

Romans offers so much wisdom to us—if we let it unfurl itself rather than conforming it to our own agendas. Our biggest problem in reading the letter is that we come to it already knowing what it says. Or so we think, anyway.

How will we know when we're reading it well?

We will know when our Christian communities are united. When Christian identity is more accurate than political affiliation in predicting our actions and convictions.

We will know when we evaluate every action by the Jesus story: are we living in such a way that our own self-sacrifice is giving life to our neighbors?

We will know when we trust God. Trust that God has been faithful to scripture in the work of Jesus. Trust that God has not made a mistake by including the people who seem to be the greatest sinners into the community of God's people. Trust that God's name receives greater praise from a motley group of worshippers than from a monolithic group of people just like us.

Even if we are the "believers."

CHAPTER TWO

Romans 1:1–17: Introducing Romans

Not a Collection of One-Liners

I try to live up to the boast emblazoned on my favorite t-shirt: "I only listen to the Mountain Goats." But every now and then, I allow myself a dalliance with other music during my morning run. "Siri, play 'Rock Classics' on Spotify," and then I'm off to the races. Most of the classics coming through my earbuds have a home somewhere deep in my memory. I find myself singing along to lyrics that I had forgotten I ever knew.

But one day, I had the opposite experience. The opening bars of "Down on the Corner," a simple yet memorable bassline, came forth. These had been seared into my memory from the days when my Creedence Clearwater Revival Greatest Hits CD was in regular rotation.

It started well enough. I had the opening lines right on the tip of my tongue.

But my stockpile of memorized "Down on the Corner" lyrics quickly ran out. After a line or two, I found that I didn't know almost any of the words. And for good reason.

Even translated through my high-fidelity earbuds, the lyrics were basically incomprehensible—a blur of "somethingsomething-something" punctuated by "Down on the corner, out in the street, somethingsomething band flinging nickels at your feet." (If you Google the lyrics, you'll find out that the line there at the end is, allegedly, "Bring a nickel, tap your feet." Even the few words I thought I understood were incorrect.)

As the song went on, I had a few anchors I could come back to. I had a bit of the setting. There were one or two spots that were clear in my mind (even if my supposed clarity was, in fact, actual fog). And there were a lot of blank spaces. Which, to be honest, makes it very difficult to hold together the narrative sweep of the song.

I imagine that Romans is somewhat like "Down on the Corner" for most of us. We remember a few one-off lines, but they're swimming in a haze of connecting lyrics that we've never been able to (or taken the time to) get our minds around.

Case in point: the infamous "Romans Road of Salvation." Those of you from my youth-group generation will remember this one—a collection of verses we used to tell the story of sin and salvation. "For all have sinned and fall short of the glory of God." Somethingsomethingsomething, "While we were yet sinners Christ died for us," somethingsomething. "The wages of sin is death but the free gift of God is eternal life in Christ Jesus our Lord," somethingsomethingsomething. "If you confess with your mouth Jesus is Lord and believe in your heart that God raised him from the dead you will be saved." Or something.

Yes, we kids knew a bunch of important verses, but in that vast ocean of somethingsomethingsomething, the thread was lost. We couldn't make out the true shape of what we were looking at. At times, theological 'maps' like the Romans Road actually kept us from being able to see what was in front of us. Our eyes were drawn to certain landmarks, keeping us from taking stock of a larger whole. The road we traveled obscured our view.

I'm not claiming to have some sort of Bible scholar key that will magically unlock Romans for the first time. Instead, I'm inviting us all to attend to what's before us, what we can see if we're willing to take the time to look.

Here's a way to get started. You know how when your teachers were droning on and on about how to write an essay, they'd tell you to write an opening paragraph? And you know how that paragraph was supposed to be a preview of coming attractions with a thesis statement and an indication of where the argument is going? Whoever it was that said such things to you, well, they didn't make it up. People have been doing that sort of thing for a long, long time.

Romans is a letter, not an essay, but ancient letters had similar conventions. There would be an opening portion where the sender identified himself or herself, and identified the recipient. Usually, you got a sense of the relationship by how each party was described. The ways that the author elaborated on their own/their recipients' identity would let you know what was coming. Was it a love letter? Was it a demand from a superior to an inferior? Was it a request from a peer? You could know the subject matter even if you couldn't yet nail down the exact content.

Here's a quick example from another one of Paul's letters. He opens his missive to the Galatians like this: "Paul. An apostle. Not sent by a human commissioning or human agency, but through Jesus Christ" (Galatians 1:1). Gosh. Defensive much? Well, that's the point. He is going to spend the first third of the letter arguing about the legitimacy of his mission.

He also goes on to describe the work of Jesus: he gave himself to rescue us from the present evil age (Galatians 1:4). This will be a major theme in the letter: how God rescues us in Christ, what we're rescued from, and how the Galatians are actually returning to the slavery that the gospel undoes.

In Romans, the stage is set with a little less drama but no less flourish. Paul elaborates on his own identity and his mission by describing Jesus's death itself in barest outline. But he locates this within a broader narrative. He tells the readers where Jesus, and his story, come from. He tells of the Spirit's work in raising Jesus from the dead. And, crucially, he tells us about the community that this work forms.

Rooted in scripture, enacted by the life-giving power of the Spirit, embracing the Gentiles: all of this is the good news that Paul brings to the Romans. This is the somethingsomethingsomething that holds together the fragments that stick in our memories.

Scripture's Gospel: Romans 1:1–7

As Paul provides us with a preview of coming attractions, at the forefront of his mind is the good news ("gospel") which "God had promised earlier through His prophets in the sacred writings" (Romans 1:2). In no other letter does Paul play the scripture card so early. And in no other letter does Paul come close to citing the Bible more often than he does in Romans. Romans contains approximately half of the scriptural citations found in the thirteen New Testament letters bearing Paul's name. *Half.*

Knowing this, one of the best postures we can adopt when coming to this letter is to ask the question, "How should we be interpreting the Bible?" Hint: excited Paulinist Daniel eagerly flipping to Romans 8:28 to prove he's right about predestination was probably doing it wrong. (Actually, I was so close to being right I should have been bowled over by what I found. Stay tuned for that coming attraction.) In fact, one of the most important purposes of Romans is to advocate for a Christian community in which people who know they have the right answers live together with other people who do not. (Those other Christians, by the way, also know that they have the right answers).

I was totally convinced that it didn't really matter if my theology made me a jerk. Maybe—just maybe—my confidence was misplaced. Maybe Romans *wasn't* written to be a one-stop-shop for procuring the "right answers."

So what exactly *does* Paul say Romans is about? What is the good news that he proclaims? Here it is (1:3–6):

God's son.
Physically born in the line of David.

Appointed God's Son at his resurrection, by the Spirit's power.
Jesus Christ. Our Lord.
The Lord who sent gifted apostles to wrap up the Gentiles into
God's family through their own faithful obedience to him.
The Lord whose name is made great by bringing in these people
who formerly were strangers.

This opening salvo gives us a roadmap of what to keep our eyes on as
we read the rest of the letter.

First, Paul establishes the deep scriptural and historical roots of
his message. Practically, this means that God's promises to the Jewish
people of a coming messiah have been fulfilled in Jesus. Jesus's physical descent and God's promises to Jesus's ancestors matter. Jesus's
Jewishness matters. They matter especially in this moment when the
Jewish people have largely rejected him as messiah.

Second, Jesus comes into the fullness of his promised power
and enthronement in a completely unexpected way. He receives the
Spirit's anointing, as David did. He takes on a new relationship to
God as God's image-bearing son, as the kings of old had done. But
Jesus receives these things after his death when God raises him from
the dead.

This is not just about Jesus. It's about the whole of cosmic reality.
The "resurrection of the dead" that Jesus experienced is the turning of
the ages. It's where the old age of sin and death passes away and the
new age of eternal life dawns. Jesus didn't come to rule over "the old
age," take a throne in Jerusalem, establish a people on earth, and then
pass from it forever. He came to establish the new age, the new creation
itself. His rule is over the entirety of the cosmos. He has ushered in the
days of the new heavens and the new earth.

By being crowned king at his resurrection, Jesus stepped into a
lordship that is larger than the roots from which he came. He is, as he
was accused of being at his death, "king of the Jews." But he is also,
through his resurrection, crowned "king of the Gentiles" as well. This,
then, is the tension hidden in Paul's opening words in Romans. It is the

paradoxical claim that the only way to honor God's commitment to the Jews is by creating a people who consist of both Jews and Gentiles.

This is how to honor the name of God, and God's appointed Messiah. This is what it means for scripture to be fulfilled.

And all of that is the gospel. All of it. Not just Jesus dying for our sins. (Notice that Paul doesn't say anything about Jesus's death on the cross here.) Not just the arrival of the Jewish Messiah. But also, this Messiah's heavenly coronation and the establishment of a people who are faithfully obedient. The good news is not good news if people are not brought in from outside. It is only good news when it creates people who are willing to form a unique kind of community. A community that is a foretaste of the eternally diverse, eternally faithful people of God.

That's what Paul tells us the gospel is in his opening salutation. In fact, it's all wrapped up in his self-description. As an apostle, as one sent by God to preach—this is what his message is. This is his life, his identity. And given its placement in Romans, it's a good bet that this is what the entire letter will be about as well.

The Thesis Statement (So They Say): Romans 1:16–17

I've gone and made this big deal about Romans 1:1–7. Now if you pick up virtually any other commentary, scholars will tell you that the best place to look for the "thesis statement" of Romans is a few verses later, Romans 1:16–17. What can I say? Everyone else in the world has a right to be wrong.

Well, I could say that. But Romans taught me that God wants to create communities of people who can live together in common worship of Jesus despite their theological differences. So let's see if these two perspectives can't be drawn together.

In the intervening verses, Paul talks about wanting to go to Rome to preach the gospel (1:11–14). This means he's talking about the exact same thing that we just covered in verses 1–7: who he is and how that's connected to his message. Then, in verses 16–17, aka the "thesis statement," he says:

> I am not ashamed of the gospel, for it is the power of God for salvation to everyone who has faith—to the Jew first and also to the Greek. For the righteousness of God is revealed in it from faith unto faith, just as it is written, 'The Righteous One will live from faith.'

The opening lines of the letter provide a roadmap for interpreting these verses. In Romans 1:2, Paul said that his gospel was proclaimed through the scriptures. This is the first scriptural citation in Romans. Moreover, Paul said that scripture was about Jesus, David's son, who was raised from the dead by the power of the Spirit. This provides strong evidence that when Paul cites Habakkuk 2:4, "the righteous (or just) will live from faith," he is talking about Jesus himself. Jesus is "the Righteous One." The promise that the Righteous One "will live," then, is a prophecy that has been fulfilled in Jesus's resurrection. The gospel message Paul preaches is, he says in verse 16, "the power of God for salvation." He has already told us (1:4) that God's power, through the Spirit, was what raised and enthroned Jesus.

Romans 1:2–4 shows us how to interpret Romans 1:16–17. It invites us to understand that the heart of Paul's gospel message is God's powerful work in raising Jesus from the dead. It is a power available to all people (1:16). This becomes a massive theme that drives chapters 6 through 8. And when we say "all people," we need to remember that Paul was a two-kinds-of-people-in-the-world kind of guy. There were Jews and there were not-Jews. Jesus came for both. Just like Paul said a few verses earlier (1:3–7).

The tight connections between the opening paragraph of the letter and these two verses that form its "thesis statement" allow us to put a few other things in place. For instance, what does "righteousness of God" mean here? This phrase basically means that God has done the right thing. We might well ask by what standard we mere mortals could judge whether God had acted rightly. Paul's answer seems to be the standard of God fulfilling God's own promises, as found in scripture. What is the content of those promises? It's the arrival of a risen Messiah who is lord over both Jews and Gentiles. When Paul says in Romans 1:5 that the faithful obedience of the nations is for "his name's sake," this is what he means. God's reputation depends on the inclusion of the Gentiles. Under the lordship of this risen Messiah.

The gospel reveals the righteousness of God by putting on display for the world the surprising manner in which God has been faithful to God's promises.

Taken together, verses 1–7 and 16–17 also show us the movement of God's work in the lives of people. There's a recurring preposition in the Greek, *eis*, that means "unto." Those sent with the message carry it "*unto* the obedience of faith"; the gospel is the power of God "*unto* salvation for everyone who has faith"; God's righteousness is revealed "*unto* faith." Notice that each time the goal of the movement is faith.

Faith (Greek *pistis*) isn't just thinking the right things. We see that the first time the word appears in Romans. Paul is looking for faith that works: the obedience of faith (*pistis;* 1:5). By the time we get through with Romans, we'll be wanting to translate "faith" using the word "trust." It's not just internalized thoughts, but beliefs that manifest in actions. It's handing ourselves over to God. It's acting in certain ways because we believe that God will honor our trusting obedience with newness of life.

This brings us back to Jesus.

Jesus in Romans is the entrée for the rest of us into the new-creation family of God. He opens this path by walking it himself. He becomes the first-born son of God at his resurrection. And it all starts with trust. Jesus himself is faithful to God. Entrusts himself to God. Even to the point of death. The death and resurrection of Jesus are where the faithfulness of humanity and the righteousness of God meet. God does what is right by giving resurrection life and an eternal kingdom to the Messiah who was faithful to the point of death.

This is what it means when Paul says in 1:17 that the righteousness of God (i.e., God's faithfulness to what God promised in scripture) is revealed in the gospel (i.e., the arrival of the messianic king, enthroned at his resurrection, to rule over Jews and Gentiles) from faith (i.e., Jesus's faithfulness) unto faith (i.e., the response of people in faithful obedience). This is what the scripture promised (Habakkuk 2:4): The Righteous One (Jesus, who did what was right) will live (be honored by God with resurrection life) from faith (out of his faithfulness to the point of death).

In the introduction, I mentioned how early Jewish people read the Bible: if God spoke in the Bible, and we're the people of God, and God has acted now in some incredible way, then this thing we're seeing among us here and now must be what God was talking about there and then. The present determines the meaning of the past. The gospel determines the meaning of Old Testament scripture (at least to a point—stay tuned for Romans 9–11).

Put together Romans 1:1–7 with Romans 1:16–17 and you'll discover what the epistle is about: God.

It's about the God who is faithful to send a Messiah and honor this faithful one with resurrection life in order to create a worldwide family walking in obedient faithfulness. That's a lot of faithful. It's a letter about a God who cannot be separated from scriptures which cannot be separated from the Messiah who cannot be separated from his people. Yes, even the family of God is required for God to be fully faithful. The righteousness of God depends on us.

What God Is Up To

Back when I had my you-should-probably-talk-to-your-therapist-about-that obsession with Romans 8:29, I was so close to the heart of Romans that I should have run into it, even if against my will. Because that verse tells us that what God did for Jesus in the resurrection, God also does for us when we join ourselves to this gospel. Jesus was "set apart" (Greek *horizo*) as the son of God at his resurrection (Romans 1:4). God "set us apart beforehand" (Greek *pro + horizo,* the word that's usually translated "predestined") to be conformed to Jesus's image: that's how he gets to be the firstborn among many brothers and sisters (Romans 8:29). And we get to be God's sons and daughters, too.

This is what predestination means.

God isn't in the business of creating people who know the one right answer.

God is in the business of creating a family.

It's corporate before it's individual. It's about being in relationship to God and each other before it's about having the right answers.

That family begins with Jesus. It's the family that renews what was lost when the image-bearing Adam was faithless to God. It's renewed by the image-bearing second Adam, Jesus, who was faithful to God and received God's faithfulness in return. (Paul will say all this in Romans 5:12–21).

As Paul tells it, the story of God is the story of the Jewish scriptures, which is the story of Jesus, which is the story of us. Romans is an extended dance on this web of interconnection. It will show us how Jesus as the display of God's righteousness leads to an affirmation of Jewish priority as well as Gentile inclusion into one new family of God (Romans 1–4). It will morph into a depiction of how Jesus as a second Adam figure inaugurates a new creation that we all are joined to when we are united to him (Romans 5–8). Then comes the heart of the matter: what does it say about God, when the people who are acknowledging Jesus's lordship consist more of Gentiles than Jews (Romans 9–11)? A final push shows what life together, for a Jewish-plus-Gentile people of God, should look like (Romans 12–16).

Many of us have grown up with an individualistic salvation model and the idea that faith is a personal choice about our personal relationship with God. But to understand Romans, it's critical we cling to what Paul tells us early in chapter 1: the gospel is only good news insofar as God, scripture, Jesus, *and the people of the earth* are in harmony.

For God to be righteous, a certain kind of people must be formed. A people consisting of Jew and Gentile. A people who show off through their faithful obedience the transformative power of God's life-giving Spirit. The people of God are the proclamation as much as Jesus himself is. The Gentile's faithful obedience is no less necessary than Jesus's.

This is why Romans had to be written. It's the people. They're off kilter. And it's calling into question whether God is, in fact, as righteous as Paul claims.

CHAPTER THREE

Romans 1:18–2:29: We're in this Together

"Everything [By Which I Mean You People] Has Gone to Crap"

While the latter half of Romans 1 invites us to the sacred, hoary depths of time, back to the creation of the world, your current tour guide wants to take a quick detour to another place that has profoundly shaped each of our hearts: elementary school. You're welcome.

Whether in the cafeteria or out on the playground, in the classroom or in the hallways, school is where children develop deep, incisive discourse for establishing a sense of self in relation to others. I think especially of the biting taunt, "I know you are, but what am I?" And its more sophisticated cousin, "I'm rubber, you're glue, whatever you say bounces off me and sticks to you." (Science, my friends.)

In addition to committing the eighth deadly sin of being annoying, these sorts of jeers are crazy-making for another reason. Listening in from the outside, it is patently obvious that they will simply escalate the tensions that prevent everyone from getting what they want. These are feeble attempts to win back control and to deflect the painful words that strike against who we want to be. They are words that virtually ensure we will continue to miss out on belonging. To be seen and known and heard—and loved.

As grownups, we engage in more complicated and subtle ways of playing these sorts of games. Accusing. Name-calling. Defensive retaliation. Sometimes, we do this in the face of individual slights. It's more socially acceptable in public. When we're defending the borders of our tribe against The People Who Are Not Like Us.

And that's where we are in Romans 1–2. Two groups of people. Generations of distrust and prejudice built up between them. Solidified by religious conviction as much as by politics and bloodshed. Jews and Gentiles. Which is to say, "The people of God," and "the not-people of God." Which is to say, all of humanity.

Paul says that his gospel message comes in accordance with the Jewish scriptures, from the Jewish people, to engulf the Gentiles as well: "To the Jew first and also to the Greek" (Romans 1:16). By the time the letter ends we will see that his heartfelt conviction is that only a worshiping community consisting of both Jews and Gentiles can appropriately manifest the saving work God has done through Jesus (Romans 15:1–12). But to get there, he is going to have to knock down the walls of tribal loyalty and prejudice. And to join Paul on his journey, we're going to need a little bit of "I know you are and so am I."

As a Jew himself, Paul is asking the most of his own people. He has to. He is going to the farthest reaches of the world, inviting strangers into the house, and changing the house rules to accommodate them. Spoiler alert! Nobody likes having the house rules changed.

My own family has a wonderfully, joyfully grumpy friend we call Mr. Richard. Whenever someone attempts to do something completely untoward, such as bringing a side dish to go with something Mr. Richard is cooking, he lays down the law with two simple words: "My house!" If you want to mess up your own meals with these "side dishes" of yours, go ahead. But not here.

If you want to live your life without the law that God gave Moses as your guide, that's your business. Until you come into my house, where the house rule is the law of Moses. Make that the law of God. Given by God's own hand. Written by God's own finger on Mt. Sinai.

If you want to be faithful to the God who sent the Jewish Jesus in fulfillment of the Jewish scriptures, you need to keep the law.

The distinction between Jew and Gentile is not just a matter of hundreds of years of divergent tradition. It is the very dividing line of God's own word, inscribed by God's own finger, on tablets of rock. Flexible? Not really. This is the very definition of something being written in stone. "My house!"

All this to say: if Paul wants to create a community of Jews and Gentiles where they worship God with one voice and live together in holistic, faithful obedience—but without requiring Gentles to adopt the house-rules of Judaism—he has a lot of work to do. So Paul enters into character in the latter half of Romans 1. He steps fully into an assumed Jewish identity and talks about the failures of "them": the ones who reject the revelation of God. The Gentiles.

The World Gone Wrong: Romans 1:18–32

Romans 1:18–32 is built on what nerds sometimes refer to as the "decline of civilization" framework. It was a common way that ancients talked about why the world is so messed up. In fact, Paul is likely recycling material from another Jewish book, *The Wisdom of Solomon* (which is included in the Apocrypha). Paul's rendering starts with an overall interpretive cue: the reason for the story that follows is that people suppress the truth of what they know about God. What should people know about God? At least this: God is God. God's creation is not God (1:20). Since people, apparently, couldn't handle that, God let them do what they wanted, and they end up worshiping creatures rather than the creator (1:23). You know how a few paragraphs ago we were talking about Paul's hope of creating a worshiping community of both Jews and Gentiles? The church we so casually walk into on a Sunday is (supposed to be) nothing less than the new-creation restoration of humanity from its primal failure. We worship the creator.

The decline-of-civilization narrative is told as an anti-creation narrative with allusions to Genesis 1. There is a creator; then people worship the various beasts and birds and creepy crawly things that fill the earth (see Genesis 1:21, 25). Then there is the dishonoring of the pinnacle of God's creation, embodied, divine-image-bearing humanity (Romans 1:24). The chapter concludes with a litany of vices practiced by those who have rejected God. All that should be condemned is instead celebrated and approved. By the idolaters. By the people who don't know God. By the Gentiles.

This is Paul the Jew articulating the perspective of his people. Not to disagree with the content so much as to disagree with the implication. That's what comes next.

Same-Sex Sex

But before we get there, there's one more thing I have to deal with from that decline-of-civilization piece. Because it sure looks like Paul takes a strong shot against same-sex intercourse. In fact, the condemnations he levels seem to function, rhetorically, as a sort of culmination of everything that's gone wrong. Whereas Genesis 1 climaxes with the creation of humans—male and female—who are to be faithful and multiply, Romans 1's anti-creation narrative reaches its nadir with women having some sort of "unnatural" sex and then men having sex with men.

It's easy to see how the church's traditional position against homosexuality can be bolstered by these verses. There is no space for a full argument here (you can check out my essay "The Moral Vision of LGBTQ Inclusion: Community, Cross, New Creation" for that[1]). But as we navigate this possible challenge to full inclusion of LGBTQI+ Christians in the life of the church here are a few things to consider.

---

[1] J. R. Daniel Kirk, "The Moral Vision of LGBTQ Inclusion: Community, Cross, New Creation," in *A Scribe Trained in the Kingdom of Heaven: Essays on Christology and Ethics in Honor of Richard B. Hays* (ed. David M. Moffitt and Isaac Augustine Morales; New York: Lexington Books/Fortress Academic, 2021), 197–216.

First, LGBTQI+ Christians who want to both be included in the church and coupled with same-sex partners are not God-denying idolaters, but worshippers of Jesus. Paul's narrative in Romans 1 doesn't fit our contemporary situation.

Second, we need to remember that Romans is teaching us how to read scripture. It is about the Jewish Messiah, raised from the dead, who exercises lordship over all people. This creates a surprising community that includes not only those who had the law (Jews) but also those who neither had it nor adopted it (Gentiles). What happens when we take that sort of posture with respect to LGBTQI+ Christians? Like the first-century Gentiles, we have a group of people who don't conform to what the established community believes God's law demands. Like the first-century Gentiles, LGBTQI+ Christians are present in the worshiping community of Israel's God, honoring Jesus as Messiah and fully contributing to the life of the church. LGBTQI+ Christians show all evidence of having the gifts and, more importantly, the fruit of the Spirit. All of us cry out to God, "Abba, Father." This makes us all members of the same family; we are siblings.

If the measures that Paul uses throughout Romans to declare the Gentiles members of God's family are correct, then the case is strong for full and unfettered inclusion of LGBTQI+ Christians in the life of the church today. Jesus is the resurrected son—so all who cry out to God as Father are his siblings. Jesus is raised by the Spirit's power—so all who walk by the Spirit share in his resurrection life and sonship. The resurrected Jesus is Lord over all, Jews and Gentiles—which makes him all the more Lord over the various flavors of Jews and Gentiles who have been united to him. In short, the presence of LGBTQI+ couples in our churches invites us to reread scripture like Paul taught us to. It calls us to recognize that belonging to the family of God is the good news with which God has already embraced untold numbers of Jesus followers who are also LGBTQI+.

But (I can hear the argument now), this isn't just a rule or a story. It's about CREATION. Creation culminates with male and female as the image of God and designed for procreation. It's a fair reply, and one that tracks with Paul's argument in Romans 1.

My response is to keep coming back to this: Paul will be teaching us how to read scripture in this letter. And reading scripture rightly is not a matter of deciphering the original design of creation and using that as our guide to what the Bible teaches. It's a matter of finding our eyes focused on the gospel of the crucified and risen Christ. In light of this, it is important to remember that there's something more important than creation. It is, perhaps, Paul's most all-encompassing theological category: "new creation." It is the renewal of all things. It begins with Jesus as a second Adam.

For Paul, *new* creation trumps *first* creation, displacing its weaknesses and failures while restoring its beauty and glory. The implication is that Jesus (the second Adam) and the new creation that lies ahead—where people neither marry nor are given in marriage (per Jesus)—are our guides in a way that the first creation can no longer be. In this new creation, Jew and Greek no longer define the world. There is no longer male and female (Galatians 3:28). In this world, first-creation rules and assumptions about sex have to be carefully reevaluated. If, there is no longer "male and female" (a clear allusion to Genesis 1:26–27) then what further basis is there for mandating "male and female" for sexual coupling? In new creation theology, the one remaining requirement would seem to be that both partners be "in Christ."

There is much more that needs to be said. But at the very least it's vital to acknowledge that we have wounded each other deeply in conversations about sexuality. Whatever else we might say or conclude, if we are using Romans to inflict those wounds rather than to heal them, then we are still a long way from reading the letter aright.

The Messed-Up World: The Jewish Part

In telling the Jewish story of how the Gentiles have messed up the world, Paul's purpose is neither to deny the facts nor to gloat about them. Rather, he is pointing out that his own people, the Jews, also are guilty: "Therefore you are without excuse—every one of you who judge" (Romans 2:1). God's mercy isn't found in giving the law, but in allowing people to repent (2:4).

Oh yeah, and don't miss the part where the final judgment is going to be based on works, not whether you had a conversion experience (2:5–6, 2:13). And not just here. Every (and I mean every) New Testament text that talks about the final judgment asserts that this reckoning is based on works. Now we start to see why "the obedience of faith" (1:5) is Paul's touchstone! But to do so, we have to clear out the somethingsomethingsomething haze that might have created a false confidence about the terrain.

One thing that "the New Perspective on Paul" helped us see was that Paul's critiques about his religious heritage weren't based on the idea that Jews work for salvation while Christians just sit back and receive a gift. Remember: Paul works backward from Jesus to what came before. The "problem" with Judaism, then, is that it does not recognize the grace of God that has come in Christ and how that redefines what faithful action (works) looks like. The celebration of the gospel is not about being released from all moral obligations but being free from the law of Moses as the definitive description of what faithfulness looks like as part of the people of God. We'll keep coming back to these observations, especially as we make our way through Romans 3, 7 and 10. Paul can turn the "works" standard in many different directions. To his Jewish compatriots, he says that the law is not enough. Doing what God desires is required. This, Paul says, is where his fellow Jews have fallen short.

Jews? All of Us?

At the end of chapter 2, Paul makes a rhetorical move that's more challenging and dangerous than rejecting Judaism's house rules. He doesn't deny that keeping God's commandments or being circumcised are critical to the identity of the people of God. Instead, he reinterprets what these beloved, sacred, God-given symbols mean. The external markers of the Jewish people are spiritualized. Circumcision that matters isn't performed with a knife; it isn't visible. Instead, it's done by the Spirit (2:28–29).

Uncircumcised Gentiles can qualify as members of the "circumcised" community of God's people. It's one thing to say, with Deuteronomy 10:16 and Jeremiah 4:4, that physically circumcised people should also show "heart circumcision" through their obedient faithfulness to God. It's another thing altogether to say that heart circumcision is, itself, sufficient.

The law isn't meant to keep a people marked out as separate. Instead, people who are faithful to God mark out where the law of God is at work (2:26–27). Circumcision had been the external sign that the Jews were God's law-keeping people. Circumcision was the tip of the … no, wait … Circumcision was the law-keeping action that symbolized obedience to the whole law.

Paul has just redefined both.

Not only that. He's redefined Jew. "He is a Jew who is one in the hidden place" (2:29). Romans 1:18–2:29 not only levels the playing field by proclaiming that Gentiles and Jews are equally guilty, are equally in need of God's mercy and equally require transforming power to live as God desires, it also radically redefines what it means to be the people of God—which is to say, what it means to be Jewish.

Paul claims to adhere to the traditional Jewish rules about circumcision and faithful obedience to God. But he has simultaneously redefined circumcision as the work of the Spirit (the one who raised Jesus from the dead) and the standards of obedience itself ("law-keeping" is now seen in the obedience of faith). The contours of the gospel outlined in Romans 1:1–7 provide the content by which Paul redefines traditional Jewish standards of faithfulness to God.

This is what I meant when I said that Paul was rewriting the house rules. It's bold. And shocking. And raises a lot more questions than it answers.

For instance, can Paul really say God has been faithful to the promises made to the Jewish people if "Jew" is now redefined to include a bunch of people God didn't make the promise to in the first place? And isn't all this just a big work-around for the greatest problem of all: most Jews simply aren't buying what Paul's selling? We'll have to wait a few chapters to get at that second question. But he'll start to tackle the first as we come to Romans 3.

CHAPTER FOUR

Romans 3: The Faith of God

Righteous God, Messed-Up World

It would be difficult for me to enumerate all the gifts that the Marvel Cinematic Universe (MCU) has bestowed. From "Hey! Let's spend our COVID lockdown watching the MCU movies in order of their internal timeline!" to the next month's, "I know! We can watch all the MCU movies in the order they came out!" to the Very Academic Dissertation on Captain America as the wielder of "America's [butt] ..." well ... okay. So maybe we're getting what we deserve with this one.

But another gift from Marvel is a character type it's brought to the fore. Although largely absent from western, Christianized culture, the trickster is a deeply familiar figure in global literature. In the MCU, the trickster is the god Loki, a riff on the character of the same name from Norse mythology. But we find the character type everywhere. The Coyote trickster features prominently in many different North American First Nations cosmologies. In Greek myths, *Hermes plays the trickster*. The Spider (Anansi) is a trickster from West African folklore.

Tricksters are murky characters. Sometimes, we cheer for them. Other times, we want to see them locked up. Although they usually aren't all-powerful gods, they are typically much stronger than humans. Basically, they have just enough power to mess things up very, very badly.

Why have people across so many times and places felt compelled to create Lokis? Because tricksters provide a way to talk about the world gone wrong—devastating earthquakes, deadly animals, weak and destructive people—while holding onto hope that there is still a God (or gods) who are good and powerful and care about us humans.

Much like Satan in the book of Job, tricksters help explain how the great gods can still be considered great in light of the harsh realities that mar our world.

As we can see, people have been wrestling with the problem of evil for a long time.

I've called this chapter "The Faith of God." I might have named it "God's not Loki." To start, Paul has a problem. It's a big problem. For Paul, the goodness of God is not an abstract concept. He doesn't talk about God as "good." He talks about God as "just," as "faithful." These are renderings of a God who is in relationship with people, who is bound by promise and obligation.

In this story, God is not free. Because God has given up freedom in favor of being bound to Israel. Through Scripture. Through covenant. Through promises spoken by the prophets.

And here's Paul, trying to have his cake and eat it, too. On the one hand, he's saying that God is faithful and righteous. On the other, he's claiming that this faithfulness requires the inclusion of the Gentiles. And right in the middle is the problem of Israel. Jews, as a whole, have not accepted the story of Jesus crucified as God's promised messiah.

One might be forgiven for thinking that Paul makes matters worse by wrapping up chapter 2 with a redefinition of what it means to be a circumcised Jew: any old human who has the Spirit and acts in a way that's pleasing to God. How can God still be considered faithful if God's work of salvation is leaving the Jewish people behind? It raises Job-type questions of God's justice and fairness. If this Jesus is Messiah, how is God not some trickster? Is Loki at work here? Romans 3 is Paul's first pass at addressing that problem.

God's Justification by Faith

His answer is justification by faith. God's justification. By God's faith. Let me explain.

In Romans 3:1–3, Paul says that the Jews have the great benefit of being "entrusted" with the oracles of God. Then, he asks whether any Jewish "faithlessness" would nullify God's "faithfulness."

Each of those words in quotation marks comes from the same Greek root (*pist-*). It means "faith" or "faithful" or "trust." Like this: They were entrusted (Greek: *episteuthesan*) but untrustworthy (*epistesan*). God didn't violate God's trust (*pistin*). Or: They were enfaithed but proved faithless. That doesn't negate God's faith, which is to say, God's relationship with God's people by faith from first to last. And when I say "from first," I mean, "from God." God entrusts the people with work. This began at creation: filling the earth, subduing it and exercising dominion over it. And God calls the people to trust, to act in ways that seem crazy to the surrounding world (Don't work one day per week!) or to wait patiently for God to act. There's a mutuality here that we sometimes miss in our well-intentioned desire to put everything into the hands of God. God's plans require human fidelity. And God's fidelity should show itself with humans receiving God's promises.

To make his point about God's faithfulness, Paul draws on scripture. In Romans 3:4 he quotes a Greek translation of Psalm 51:4, which imagines God standing trial. God wins. This is what "justification" means. It's being vindicated in a judicial case. Paul's claim here is that God's truth will endure beyond all human lies. God will be faithful. God will stand by what God has spoken and will be justified by God's own words. This is an ancient version of what later philosophers would call theodicy: the justification or vindication of God.

Here, we have the first mention of justification by faith in Romans. And it's God who is justified. Because God has kept faith with Israel. God has done what is right.

So What About the Jews?

Paul's bold claim comes at a price (Romans 3:5–8): he has created a gap between God and the people of Israel to whom God is supposed to be faithful. Worse, he has tied God's justification to the people's failure (3:5), as if a dark backdrop were needed to make the brightness of God's truth visible (3:7).

So Jews have an advantage, yes—they have the words of God. And then God uses their rejection of the gospel message for God's good reason (getting the message to the Gentiles). This does not make their disobedience honorable (3:8). And it raises questions about God.

At the same time, Paul goes on to say, having access to the scriptures does not make the Jewish people holier than thou (3:9–20). Paul takes on the persona of a Jewish conversation partner to ask, "So we're better?" (3:9). The answer is an unequivocal "No." And Paul unveils a litany of biblical quotations from Psalms 5, 10, 14, 36 and 140, and Isaiah 59 to prove his point. Everyone has sinned! None are righteous! Fair enough.

But surprisingly, many of these Bible verses were originally talking about Gentiles. If redefining "circumcised Jews" as "spiritually circumcised anyones" is the shocking conclusion of chapter 2, condemning Jews as though they were blasphemous Gentiles is the surprise of chapter 3.

Here's how Paul pulls off this surprise. Even though those verses were originally speaking about Gentiles, no outsiders would have heard them. So when Paul says, "What the law says, it speaks to those who are within its bounds" (Romans 3:19), he's turning it back around onto the Jewish people. The law doesn't make the Jewish people the faithful people of God. It only shows the full extent of their need for forgiveness.

Can we just push the pause button for a second? Thanks.

We're on some pretty treacherous ground right now. History has shown us that. What we're reading is a Jewish man arguing that the Jewish God has acted in a way that his fellow Jews largely don't see as God's work. His language is strong. He is fervent in the way that people are when religious conflicts generate heated passion.

And he is heartbroken.

These are his people. He is fully convinced that God is as committed to them as God has ever been. Romans is not written to condemn the Jews, but to wrestle through the impossible scenario that God would act in a way that leaves so many of God's own beloved people behind.

The history of Christianity is filled with theological heroes who show deeply anti-Jewish tendencies. And it is littered with deadly anti-Semitism. Therefore, it is crucial to remember that the faith by which God is justified is God's keeping faith with the Jewish people, first and foremost. Anti-Semitism and anti-Judaism is antithetical to the message of Romans, God's own deep affection for the Jews, and to Paul and Jesus—both Jews to the end.

Ok. Unpause.

What Scripture Witnesses To

A second ago, I said that the law only shows how much people need to be forgiven. Well, not "only." According to Paul, the law also bears witness to something other than itself (Romans 3:21).

Remember way back in Romans 1, when we learned to read scripture as if it's talking about Jesus as the Jewish messiah, ruling over Jews and Gentiles? Yeah, that. Well, the law is part of scripture. So if you're reading those early commandments in Exodus or Leviticus or Deuteronomy just to find out what to do, or if you're using it to draw a circle around people and say that they are the people of God, you're missing the point.

What does the Law, along with the Prophets, bear witness to? Three things, as Paul tells us in Romans 3:21–22.

1. *The righteousness of God.* We've seen this before, in the "thesis statement" laid out in Romans 1:16–17: God is making good on what God promised to do for Israel. God isn't holding up some sort of external, cosmic standard. God is choosing to be

bound to Israel and to act on behalf of Israel for the sake of humanity.

2. *God's righteousness is demonstrated in Jesus's faith.* This, too, was introduced in Romans 1:16–17. Jesus's faith is his trust in God even as he went to the cross. Romans 3:25 brings these two concepts together: God puts God's own righteousness on display by offering Jesus as an atoning sacrifice through Jesus's faith(fulness).

3. *Righteousness through Jesus's faith is conferred on everyone who believes/trusts.* At the risk of sounding repetitious, we've also seen this before. In Romans 1:16–17. If Romans 1:16–17 is Paul's "thesis statement," then here Paul claims that his thesis will be supported by key passages from the Law and Prophets.

What I've just outlined gives us a laser focus on Jesus's death as the thing that saves us. Part of that happens by reading the Greek just a little differently than it has often been translated. Paul uses a Greek phrase that can be literally translated "the faith of Christ." This could mean either the faith that we have in Christ, or Christ's own faith or faithfulness.

If that grammar is hard to get your mind around, here's an illustration. In seminary, someone gave me a book entitled *The Worship of the English Puritans.* Since I was at a school that prided itself on its roots in English Puritanism, I was deeply disappointed to discover that no, this was not a book about how various Presbyterians worship the English Puritans. It was, instead, about how the English Puritans worshiped God. In the title, "Puritans" can either be the subject of the implied verb "to worship" (they are worshiping God) or the object of worship (they are worshiped by Presbyterians—which would have made for a *much* better book).

Back to Jesus. In the early 1980s, Richard B. Hays revived the argument that when Paul is talking about "the faith of Jesus Christ," he intends to communicate Christ's faith—which is his faithful obedience to God in going to death on the cross.[1] *This does not remove human faith as the appropriate response to Jesus's act of self-giving love!* But if you read through Romans and Galatians with this understanding of "the faith of Jesus Christ," the net effect is to move more of what saves us, and more of what makes God righteous, onto the work of Jesus.

It can be challenging to follow all the details of Paul's argument in Romans 3:22–26 because some of the connections he's making are lost in translation. For instance, in Greek, the noun "righteousness" (*dikaiosune*) has the same root (*dik-*) as the verb "justify" (*dikaioo*) and the adjective "just" or "righteous" (*dikaios*). Justification is what happens to someone who is just, who has acted justly.

It starts with God. God puts God's righteousness on display through the death of Jesus (3:21–22). This means that God's act of faith in giving Jesus is proof that God is just—it's the reason God is justified when God is judged (3:4).

This was one of those eye-popping realizations that made me realize that Paul's gospel was much more about Jesus than my earlier Romans Road understanding. I used to have this idea that "God's righteousness" was about God's ... well, right ... to punish people for sin. Yes, that eventually meant Jesus bearing people's punishment, but "righteousness" was a more abstract concept, something about a universal standard of action. Instead, righteousness is about God doing the right thing in relationship to Israel, which is to say, doing what God had promised in scripture. This is something God can be held accountable to.

Righteousness is being just, which is also why a verdict would be handed down to justify (vindicate) a person in court. But the big shocker for me was that God's justification by faith, no less than our own, hinges on the death of Jesus. The door swings both ways.

---

[1] Richard B. Hays, *The Faith of Jesus Christ: The Narrative Substructure of Galatians 3:1–4:11* (Grand Rapids: Eerdmans, 2002). The idea has been hotly debated, with James D. G. Dunn and E. P. Sanders, whom we mentioned earlier, taking the position that these phrases should be translated "faith in Jesus Christ" throughout Paul's writings.

Jesus Changes Everything

For Paul, the death of Jesus is a game changer. Not in the sense of changing the outcome of a game already in progress by giving one side the boost it needs. No, it's much more serious than that. According to Paul, God does not judge us based on whether we have kept the law, or even on whether Jesus came and kept it for us. Instead, Paul claims, the rules have changed entirely.

God judges based on the faithfulness that is seen in Jesus going to death on the cross. The faithfulness that God vindicates isn't keeping the law, it's this one-time act of self-sacrifice. Yes, there will be a "judgment according to works" (Romans 2:6). But those works will be the obedience that flows from entrusting ourselves to Jesus; or, better, entrusting ourselves to God in the same way that Jesus did.

This is the heart of Paul's argument that Jews and Gentiles are on the same ground, equally guilty and equally needing God's intervention to be just. This is why Paul doesn't think that Jews have a leg up when it comes to being justified. And this is why so many Jews through the ages have not been swayed by Paul's gospel. It puts the performance of the law on the back burner, rather than making it a core component of the identity of God's people.

Separating vindication in the sight of God from the law that God gave Israel is the only way that God can truly be God over both Jews and Gentiles. Occupying the space demarcated by the law makes a person a Jew, by definition. However, Paul doesn't believe that conversion to Judaism is necessary to be part of God's people. Gentiles can be children of God.

It's this commitment—that Gentiles can be God's children without converting to Judaism—that leads Paul to sum up his argument in chapter 3 by talking about the "law" of faith. We are part of the people of God because of an interwoven web of faith(fulness). God's faithfulness is seen in offering Jesus as a sacrifice. Jesus's faithfulness is seen in his willingness to be the sacrifice. We respond with faithful acceptance of Jesus's sacrifice. And all of this means no one can boast in their standing before God based on being part of the law-people. The law has a different function in the story Paul tells. It doesn't draw a line around God's people; it draws an arrow pointing to Jesus.

Pause.

Whenever we read, we are also interpreting. Whether we know it or not. And when we interpret, we fall into big patterns. Nerds refer to this as "hermeneutics." And hermeneutics very often reflect our core commitments.

We can see this pretty clearly in our own polarized society. Most of us have news sources that we trust to interpret the world. And we have an equally long list of those we don't trust. These reflect our core commitments—especially to our tribes.

What do we value? What do we want to be true? What narratives do we believe? What do we entrust ourselves to? Where is our faith? What story do we tell ourselves about how the world works? What kind of world do we hope to see come to pass? What communities do we belong to already? What kind of community do we want to be part of? The answers to all of these questions, whether spoken or unconscious, impact how we interpret how we read and what we hear.

Unpause.

Let's take stock of this massive thing Paul is asking of his fellow Jews, the profound demand he's placing on us and the enormous transformation he's undergone. He's asking us all to start from The Event. To trust that the death and resurrection of Jesus is The Thing that God has done. The world-changing thing. The cosmic answer to the primal promise.

What Paul is asking of people who read the scriptures of Israel, especially Jewish people, is something like asking a modern American to flip-flop their news loyalty from either *The New York Times* or Fox News to the other one. Only harder. He wants everyone to go back and reinterpret everything they thought they knew about the world in light of the death and resurrection of Jesus. Paul is summoning us to read the Bible differently—not as "timeless" documents showing how God's people are to act, but as a marker written in an earlier time that shows the way to something, and someone, coming later.

How difficult is this to do? For Paul's fellow Jews, this was a daunting prospect. But even people who claim that Jesus is the Messiah too often fall into the trap of reading the Bible to validate our insider identity.

We read biblical stories of a chosen nation and anointed kings and wars waged in the name of God—and believe that reenacting their scenes is part of our Christian birthright. Throughout the millennia in various parts of the world, Christianity became entwined with empire, and those who inherited this empire-infused faith appropriated these ancient stories, adopting them as their own. They were used to claim land that belonged to others, to slaughter indigenous peoples, to their exalt leaders on the world stage—arrogant acts of violence held up as evidence of God's blessing. In short, Christian nationalism obscured the message of these stories (which, incidentally, were composed by a conquered and displaced peoples). So blinded, Christians miss the message of the stories: they highlight people's recurring shortcomings to show us that God has something else in store. A different way of life. The cross-shaped way of love.

The faith of Jesus.

We too often scour our Bibles for proof texts justifying our tribalism. We long to claim God for our own side at the expense of our neighbors—even those who call Jesus Lord, just as we do. We miss the call to make God's name known by enlarging the tent so that Jesus might be shown to be, truly, Lord of all. Not just those who are like us. "God is one," Paul tells his Jewish contemporaries (Romans 3:30). So we, the people of God, must be one as well.

When Paul says that scripture foreshadows the Jewish messiah who suffered and died, only to be raised to lordship over even obedient Gentiles, this is what he's urging us to. He wants us to carry such a firm conviction that this is, in fact, our founding story that we make it, also, the story of our life together. That we make it our core conviction.

This Jesus story then becomes our hermeneutic. It becomes our way of reading. It becomes our way of judging between right and wrong. It becomes our way of life.

This is what it means to be justified by God's faith.

CHAPTER FIVE

Romans 4:
Father Abraham?

Who Is God?

In December of 2015, controversy broke out at a renowned Christian college, making national headlines in the United States. (Spoiler alert: almost every time this happens, the institution is wrong and the person causing the controversy is faithfully following Jesus. But that's another book for another day.)

Professor Larycia Hawkins, a tenured faculty member at Wheaton College, who also happened to be a Black woman, announced that she would be donning the hijab throughout the Advent season as a sign of solidarity with Muslims facing discrimination. The context: a married couple with jihadist motivations had just killed fourteen people in San Bernardino, California. Anti-Muslim sentiment was high.

In a Facebook post, Hawkins explained her act as one of religious solidarity, showing her unity with people who worship the same God. In response, Wheaton forced her out. Hawkins ended up being upgraded from coach to first class after the University of Virginia scooped her up for a professorship. But not before she left one huge question swirling around the theological spaces she had vacated (or, more accurately, had been evicted from). Do Christians and Muslims, in fact, worship the same God?

When I was working on my PhD, I had a theology professor who was famous for saying, "When I say 'God,' what I mean is 'Father, Son and Holy Spirit.'" Can I get a quick show of hands from any Muslims out there who'd agree? Right. That would be zero. So Hawkins was wrong? Not so fast.

While we're counting noses, can I get a quick show of hands from any Biblical writer who, when they said "God," meant "Father, Son and Holy Spirit"? Still no hands. That doesn't mean that the Christian conviction about God being Trinity is wrong. It just means that it's a much more audacious claim than we sometimes realize.

What happens if we approach the question of God's identity somewhat differently? If, instead of articulating God's identities in static theological categories, we ask about the character in the story: Do we worship the creator God who is also the God of Abraham? Now the hands go up from every Christian, Muslim and Jew, from every writer of the Bible, every interpreter of the Koran, every tradent of the Torah.

Paul was a Jew, writing Romans in the city of Corinth, in the thick of the Roman Empire. A temple of Aphrodite was located on a high hill, visible from miles away. So the question "Which god are we talking about?" was in some ways much easier for him to answer.

But that makes Paul's situation all the more precarious. Because the God he's talking about is the God of Abraham, Isaac and Jacob. The God of the Hebrews. The God who brought Israel out of the land of Egypt, out of the house of bondage. These phrases capture the identity of God.

If Paul is proclaiming an act of salvation that has, somehow, not swept up the seed of Abraham, the children of Israel, then how can he still be talking about the work of the Jewish God? If Paul is redefining the identity of the people of God around faith and Jesus, what does this mean for who God is?

There's only one way around this dilemma and that's to go straight through it. In Romans 4, Paul sets about reworking the idea of Abraham as forefather. Along the way, he reconstructs the identity of Abraham's God so that it meshes perfectly with the gospel message Paul proclaims. Remember in the introduction how we talked about the rules of ancient biblical interpretation? That whole thing about what God has done in the present determining the meaning of what God did in the past? That's where we are in Romans 4.

Abraham: What Kind of Father?

Paul concluded Romans 3 with the nervy assertion that the gospel story he's telling, in which justification does not come by works of the law, nonetheless upholds and establishes the law (Romans 3:31). He also said that the law bears witness to this coming work of God (3:21). Romans 4 is showtime.

Paul begins with a question. In most Bible versions, Romans 4 opens with something like this: "What then shall we say that Abraham, our forefather according to the flesh, discovered" (NIV)?

But given the way that Paul deploys rhetorical questions in Romans and elsewhere, New Testament scholar Richard B. Hays has proposed a more likely translation: "Have we found Abraham to be our forefather according to the flesh?" The implied answer is "no."

He is our forefather in faith instead.

We can divide Romans 4 into two parts. In the first part, verses 1–15, Paul argues that Abraham's justification is just like what Paul himself proclaims: independent of circumcision, independent of the works of the law. In the second part, verses 16–25, he makes the specific connection between what Abraham believed and what Paul proclaims: God is the one who raises the dead. In order for the people of God to take on a new identity, God's identity must be understood in a fresh way as well.

Paul draws on two Old Testament characters to prove that his concept of justification is in step with Israel's scriptures. First, there is Abraham. Back in Genesis 15, Abram (as he was then known) complained to God about not having an heir from his own physical line. God responded with a promise of descendants as numerous as the stars of the sky. Abram believed this promise, and the Lord "reckoned it to him as righteousness" (Genesis 15:6). Remember that: the specific promise Abram is responding to is the numerous offspring. This will be important later.

This "reckoned righteousness" did not come from good deeds Abram had performed, but simply because he trusted what God said. In fact, I almost think that the Genesis 15:6 blessing was a "hurry up and bless him for believing before he goes and impregnates Hagar in order to try to get kids on his own" sort of thing. (Abram literally goes and impregnates Hagar in the next chapter of Genesis.) But that's not where Paul goes with it.

Paul argues that Abraham didn't work for that verdict of "righteous" that God bestowed; nor was he circumcised. Here, Paul rests his argument that uncircumcised, non-law-keeping Gentiles can also share in the blessing of justification. If not being circumcised was good enough for Abraham, it is good enough for modern-day Gentiles as well.

This is where Hays's translation of Romans 4:1 is validated. The question is, "Is Abraham our forefather *according to the flesh?*" Paul says Abraham is the ancestor of all who believe—both those who are uncircumcised and those who are circumcised (Romans 4:11–12). So the answer is "no"; Abraham is not our forefather *according to the flesh.* Instead, he is our ancestor *according to faith.* Even those who are circumcised need faith. And not just any faith, but the faith Paul is proclaiming. We'll get there in just a second.

In verses 7–8, Paul draws on his second Old Testament character, David, quoting from Psalm 32 (attributed to the king): Blessed are those whose iniquities are forgiven, and whose sins are covered; blessed is the one against whom the LORD will not reckon sin. Though this citation doesn't use the word "justification," it speaks of God's blessing coming through forgiveness and the non-reckoning of sin. In other words, justification doesn't come through the good things a person does but through God not counting the bad things a person has done.

Paul includes Abram's story from Genesis 15 and David's testimony from Psalm 32 to bear witness to the "righteousness of God" in

Romans 4. God establishes a way of righteousness and atonement for us through Jesus's death on the cross.

That atonement is equally open to Jews and Gentiles. It does not happen because of law-keeping; but the Law (Abraham's story is found in the Torah) and the prophets (the psalms were considered prophetic) bear witness to it (Romans 3:21).

Most Christians reading this book likely share Paul's basic assumption that Jesus plays a central role in God's plans to reconcile and restore the world to Godself. It is important for folks like us to take a step back and recognize that for people who don't share this starting point, Paul's interpretation of the Abraham story probably sounds … weird, at best. At worst? Maybe manipulative and disingenuous.

For instance: in Genesis 15 Abram's big gripe is that he has no physical progeny to be his heir. So God promises him an heir, and even beyond that, descendants as countless as the stars in the sky. Paul reinterprets this story about physical descendants to argue that Abraham's paternity is not, in fact, about physical conception and birth but, instead, a faith that anyone can share.

Jesus Comes First

Paul isn't being disingenuous. Like his fellow Jews, he had grown up reading and interpreting the scriptures from front to back, beginning with Genesis. This approach gave rise to various expectations of what God's final salvation might look like. But now, he has become fully convinced that the climactic act of salvation is found in the death and resurrection of Jesus. This requires him to reread the earlier stories and understand them in a new light.

The narrative of the crucified Jesus as the resurrected Lord and Messiah is the all-controlling piece in Paul's account. It is the key for reinterpreting the ancient stories of God's commitment to Israel, and for understanding why Israel largely rejects this message of salvation even as the Gentiles are accepting it.

Believing in Jesus comes first. Without that, none of the rest makes sense.

Ancient Jews, like Paul, are not the only ones who do this, by the way. Literally every time we apply the Bible to our lives or the world around us, we are giving an interpretation of the Bible based on our fundamental convictions about what it says. As often as not, this is not what the author of the biblical text was initially trying to say.

This is not bad! We are human. It is inevitable. This is simply how we read texts that we believe in. But it does mean that we have to take great care in how we tell our story, because this will shape our understanding of whether things are right or off kilter. It will influence what we praise and what we condemn. How we tell the story tells us who is in and who is out.

And ultimately, all these things shape and are shaped by our understanding of the identity of God. What kind of God would approve the various stories we tell in God's name?

Paul, one of the biblical "people of God," argues that this category actually is much broader than he and the other Jewish "insiders" had realized. Though the subsequent history shows Christians ascending to global dominance in a way that has left enduring scars on the Jewish people, at the time Paul was making a radical overture to expand the definition of those who used to be outsiders. These were people who could literally only inhabit the margins of this God's worship, the ones who, by very definition, were "sinners" (see Galatians 2:15).

The God Paul has on offer is a God whose blessings transgress the boundary markers erected by law, by tradition—and even the promises of what the future would look like. When God makes good on God's word, the results are often a surprise. This God is faithful and generous beyond all expectations.

Resurrection Faith

In the second half of Romans 4, Paul shows that the connection between Abraham and Jesus-followers is not simply a shared disposition of faith.

The blessings Paul is talking about aren't simply a divine reward for people who exercise the correct human posture. This is only one piece of the puzzle of faith. Remember what we saw in both chapters 1 and 3: God's faith(fulness), through Christ's faith(fulness) results in human faith(fulness).

There is a specific God, tied to a specific story with specific promises and specific actions, who must be the object of faith. How is it, then, that Paul connects the God of his gospel with the God of Abraham?

Resurrection.

Paul proclaims that God's resurrection power is manifested in Jesus, by the Spirit (Romans 1:4). Here, he makes the bold claim that Abraham trusted that same resurrection power—but for a different sort of life from the dead.

Abraham was probably in his eighties when God made this promise to him. Sarah was no spring chicken, either. Here's how Paul puts it, in a literal translation of the Greek: "Without becoming weak in faith, Abraham considered his body which *had already died* because he was about a hundred years old, and the *deadness* of Sarah's womb" (4:19).

This is how Paul can claim that Abraham believed in the God who gives life to the dead (4:17)—because God brought life out of Abraham's "dead body" and Sarah's "dead womb."

How do we know that the God of Abraham is the same as the God of Paul? Because this is the God who gives life to the dead. That is what this God has done at the foundational moments in Israel's story and the story of the early church. Isaac is life brought forth from the bodies of dead parents. And Jesus was raised from the dead to be enthroned as Lord over all.

This, in fact, is the conclusion that Paul draws at the end of Romans 4. That thing about Abraham believing God and having it credited to him as righteousness? The passage had a forward-looking thrust; it was written for those who believe Paul's gospel message and who will receive such a reckoning themselves (4:23–24). "These are the people who believe in the God who raised Jesus our Lord from the dead" (4:24).

Abraham's faith bears witness to the faith Paul is trying to summon up among the nations, as it points the way toward trust in the God who raises the dead with the end result being justification by faith.

The final verse of chapter 4 sums up the prior two chapters when it describes Jesus as "the one who was delivered up because of our transgressions and raised because of our justification" (4:25). Justification is God's verdict that someone is in the right. The death of Jesus is the just action, setting to rights through non-reckoning of sin. Justification is God's verdict, pronounced first on Jesus through his resurrection, and then on the rest of us.

This is where the faith of God, the faith of Jesus and the faith of humanity all come together. This is what was promised beforehand in the scriptures, what Abraham anticipates.

The God of Abraham

To lay claim to the God of Abraham is to acknowledge that the God we're talking about is a character within a certain story, who has acted in distinctive, defining ways. But we don't have to look particularly hard at the history of Jewish, Muslim and Christian relations to see that this particular story raises as many questions as it answers. Tensions are inevitable because each Abrahamic faith takes a different moment as the defining narrative lending coherence to their story.

This calls for humility. Arriving at the Christian conclusion of the story, in the life, death and resurrection of Jesus, is not a matter of waiting for what was obviously coming down the pike. Just read the Gospels. Nobody knew what was coming. The gospel is not an obvious conclusion so much as a faith-driven starting point. Those who start with a crucified and risen Messiah will read differently everything that has come before. We're going to see more of this in the coming chapters.

Moreover, commitment to this particular God should leave us cautious about where to draw the lines between insiders and outsiders.

Sometimes the people God includes are the very ones we would define as excluded "others," sinners beyond the pale. And yet God brings them in, without requiring circumcision or law-keeping—or their modern-day equivalents.

Some things we can only know after the fact. And in light of those surprises, we come to understand new names for the God we have known all along. Names like, "The God who gives life to the dead."

CHAPTER SIX

Romans 5: Stitching a Story, Beginning to End

Stories of Peace

Despite having taken hundreds of flights, I continue to cultivate an awe of flying. The height, yes. But especially the speed. Step into a tube of steel and aluminum, then reemerge hours later at the end of a trip that used to take people months to complete.

But all that joyful wonder ebbs away as the plane starts to descend. Because I know what's coming next. It starts to well up as the plane touches down. A suffocating panic.

Soon, hundreds of people will be standing up all around me and I'll be trapped. No way to get out. Welcome to the most regularly occurring setup for my anxiety attacks.

What am I afraid of? Well, I'm like most people who have panic or anxiety attacks. It turns out that the number one reason for panic attacks is ... the fear of having a panic attack.

What I want is to have control over my environment, to be able to leave whenever I choose. I'm not scared of being in a small space; I'm scared of not being able to get out of it. And of not being able to breathe. And of passing out from fear or lack of oxygen.

Anxiety is a powerful illustration of how deeply affected we are by our innate human drive to be storytellers. Our bodies respond to what our minds fear might be around the corner, connecting the dots between the present and the anticipated future. Which is really not so great when the story says, "RUN AT ALL COSTS," and I can't move a muscle. Please don't ever put me in an MRI machine. I think I would literally die.

Of course, there's an upside to this as well. If there are futures that fill us with dread and terror, there are also futures that augur peace and joy. Just as it is possible for the prospect of a frightening future to overwhelm my body as my flight-or-fight impulses go haywire, it is also possible for the vision of a welcoming future to bring eagerness or calm.

In the first half of Romans 5, Paul connects the dots between the past and the future in a way that has the power to radically transform the present. Having been justified—vindicated (i.e., in the past)—we have peace with God through Jesus (i.e., in the present; 5:1–2).

This story has a future as well. What is the future that Paul sees? What is the hope he sets our eyes on? The glory of God (5:2). Not just that we glorify God, but that we also get to be part of the awesome.

We share in it. We reflect it. We embody it. We *are* the glory of God.

Maybe that's why getting the "we" right takes up so much space in these first few chapters. If we are going to be the fullness of God's glory, we need to get the fullness of God's people into the room.

Paul goes on to connect the past, the present and the future a couple more times in these verses.

Even when we suffer, we continue to hope for glory (5:3–5). This is because suffering is part of the path of our formation. It's part of a story that God is using to bring us to a glorious ending as a certain kind of people—people of character, proven people, people of hope. The Holy Spirit (5:5) gives us confidence that our path leads to a good future gifted to us by God.

In these opening verses (5:1–5), Paul tells our story from our justification (the past) through our possession of the Spirit (the present) to glory (the future). Running throughout it all? Peace.

Not anxiety. Not panic. Not conflict. Peace.

Even if there's suffering. Even if there are a million things that simply have to be endured. Peace. With hope.

Play it Again, Paul: The Story of God's Love

We keep returning to the idea that death and resurrection so occupy Paul's vision that they transform everything else he sees. They change who humanity is as we stand before God. In a way, they make peace with God possible for the first time.

In Paul's understanding of the story, people are not "okay with God" simply by virtue of being humans, originally created in God's image. The first two and a half chapters of Romans stand against that idea. It's also not the human disposition of faith, irrespective of its object or source, that sets people on the path of peace.

Rather, according to Paul, peace with God is newly possible because God acted in faith through the faith of Jesus. And we have the opportunity to entrust ourselves to that storyline. That story promises a future that can be ours if we will take hold of its past, its founding moment, and give ourselves to it.

So Paul runs through the story a second time (5:6–11).

He reminds us of the starting point: we were weak, we were sinners. And yet. Still. Nonetheless. Christ died for us.

This is what the love of God looks like. It looks like God has enemies. And yet, God regards these enemies with kindness.

It looks like humanity is in open rebellion against God, suppressing the truth and not acknowledging God's presence and goodness. Still, God takes the initiative.

It looks like God reconciling us. The divine solution to the problem of human rebellion is, ultimately, to adopt us into God's family (see Romans 8:29). We were enemies. Nonetheless, we are God's children.

The death of Jesus accomplishes this (5:8). Jesus's blood is the basis of our vindication (v. 9). The sacrifice of Jesus's life is the act of reconciliation (5:10). This foundational act creates a new chapter in the story of God and humanity. And this story is going someplace. It is headed toward a final salvation that yet lies in the future (5:10). On the Day of Judgment there will be no wrath (5:9). At its heart, this is what justification means. It is full and final vindication when we stand before God.

In the present we live between the past of Jesus's sacrifice and the future of final salvation—this present is a place of peace because of where the story came from and where it's going. No need to worry. No need to panic. We have the confidence that God is for us because of what Jesus has done (5:11).

I can't tell you how many times I've wished that this big story would overwrite the little stories that overwhelm me day by day. Maybe that's the hardest part of living into this vision that Paul paints for us.

I wish I had an easy answer for how to let "peace with God" translate into "peace while packed in like sardines on an airplane." I don't.

But the idea that God wants peace for me is a compass of sorts. It shows me when I'm living in the fullness of what God intends for humanity as God is remaking us through the work of Jesus. It helps me know when I'm off the wagon due to my own stirring up of non-peace for myself or others. And it helps me to receive agents of peace as gifts from God. Gifts like listening prayer or mindfulness meditation. Like time in nature or leaving aside social media.

And maybe, little by little, the story of peace with God can become a big enough story to nudge out the smaller stories of non-peace that keep me up at night. Or that send me into a panic at touchdown.

Adam: Guilt and Power

In the first half of Romans 5, Paul brings his initial argument to its climax: justification by faith—God's, Christ's, ours—means that Jews and Gentiles alike have hope for salvation. In the opening chapters of Romans, the problem of sin as "guilt" is paramount.

In the second half of chapter 5, Paul introduces a new element of his argument, which he will develop through chapter 8. Here we'll discover that salvation is not only about forgiveness of guilt, but also about deliverance from enslaving powers.

Paul pulls the camera back and retells the story of salvation in a larger context that extends beyond Israel and transcends the Jewish law. He wants to show how sin takes root earlier in the story, so he goes back to Adam, the Bible's first human. As he does so, he discovers that the guilt of sin, requiring forgiveness, is not the only problem. Looming alongside it is guilt's twin: sin's power. This is what gives death its might. And this is why people need freedom.

Generations of Christians have petitioned for such relief in the old hymn "Rock of Ages," crying out, "Be of sin the double cure, cleanse me from its guilt and power." Throughout the coming chapters, we will see how the work of Jesus and the gift of the Spirit provide intertwined answers to the problems of sin's guilt and power, leading to final salvation, final vindication and life in the age to come.

It all starts with a grammatically and logically convoluted paragraph, in which Paul sets out to show us how Adam and Jesus are alike—and winds up outlining how they're different (5:12–21)! Let's see what we can make of it.

Paul argues two things in the latter half of Romans 5. First, drawing on Israel's rich scriptural traditions he asserts that Adam and Jesus are alike because each takes one particular action, the consequences of which impact all of humanity. Second, he argues that Adam and Jesus are *not* alike, because Jesus's action brings life, righteousness and freedom, whereas Adam's action brings death, sin and slavery.

Okay, Paul argues a third thing, as well. He's trying to relativize the place of the law in the saving story of God's people. The law plays a role, but not the role of savior.

Paul makes an assertion here that Adam did something, and all of us pay the price. It's not Paul's most popular idea. In fact, it's so unpopular that you won't find it in the Old Testament! But remember,

Paul is reading his scriptures in light of what he believes about Jesus. There's something he believes about what Jesus has accomplished, and he's telling the Adam story to help make the point. It's the Jesus part he's really interested in, but he's starting with Adam because he wants us to understand how this applies to everyone, not just Israel.

So, what is it that Adam did? Adam broke a commandment (which is what "transgression" means). And what's the price for the rest of us? Everyone else shares his guilt.

Even though not every person has been given a command from God and broken it, Paul still says, "All sinned" (5:12). In Greek, there are a couple of different ways of expressing things that have happened in the past. Paul uses the one-off, non-continuing verb form (*hēmarton*). It's not that Adam set a pattern and the rest of us followed. The one thing he did applies to us as well. In other words, what Adam did, we all did.

And it unleashed a reign of terror. Adam's transgression was the gateway that let sin into the world (5:12). Sin as a power that enslaved humanity. Sin as the instrument of death.

Oh, yeah. Death. That came, too. Sin brought it in tow (5:12). And death became king. Ruling over humanity, all creatures, relentlessly (5:14).

Where does the law fit into all this? Well, part of Paul's point is that it doesn't. In verses 13 and 14, Paul claims that "sin is not counted where there is no law," and there was no law before God gave the commandments to Israel.

Ok, there's one exception. God had given a commandment to Adam. He had one thing to do.

This is how Adam is the precursor to Jesus in a way that Israel under the law is not. Each of them are individuals with one specific thing to do. Adam fails. Jesus succeeds. And even though they are individuals, they represent the rest of us.

Reigning Through Jesus

Adam fails and many die. Jesus succeeds and many receive the gift of God's grace (5:15).

Adam's one sin leads to judgment and condemnation. Jesus is subjected to many transgressions against himself, and it leads to vindication (5:16).

But here's the best part. Don't miss it.

In Romans 5:17, Paul reiterates that death reigns through Adam's transgression. But he does not then set up a rhetorical "life reigns" foil. He doesn't even say that Jesus reigns. Or God. Instead, he says that the people who receive God's gift of grace, in Christ, will reign in life.

In other words, *we* reign.

If you go back to Genesis 1, you'll see that God has a purpose for humanity beyond "image-bearing" and reproducing. Our work is to rule over the creation as God would (Genesis 1:26). As Paul compares and contrasts Adam and Jesus, he catches a glimpse of humanity's glorious future. The whole point of this story is to restore and renew humanity, not leave humanness behind. This restoration of humanity includes a return to what God intended from the beginning: a divine family (to be the "image and likeness" of God is to be God's daughter or son; see Genesis 5:1–3) exercising the divine prerogative of rule.

Let's pause again.

Because if anything in the history of humanity—and Christianity in particular—has ever gone sideways, it's this idea that we are in charge of the world. It has been the seed of crusades, inquisitions and genocide. It has underpinned slavery and religious discrimination.

And not a little of the environmental degradation and ecological crisis we're facing has its origins, and ongoing justifications, here as well.

All of this comes from imitating the wrong king. It comes from taking our cues from the destructive powers of sin and death, whose rule Paul ties to the sin of Adam. This is not how God rules.

Just look at that opening chapter of Genesis. Every time you turn around, God is elevating and empowering God's creation.

"Let there be light!" is the first act of creation. Then on day four, God creates two great lights. Redundant? It might seem that way. But the lights God creates have a job to do. They will mark the day and night and the changing seasons, yes.

But there's more.

They are given the task of rule. The greater light will rule the day, the lesser will rule the night (Genesis 1:16). God divests power. The God of Genesis 1 does not want to be the sole, direct ruler of everything on the earth. God wants to empower the various parts of creation to take up their power as appropriate—and to rule like God rules.

This is not life-taking tyranny. This is life-giving generosity. God imparts power so that underlings can grow and thrive and come into their own. And a few verses later, when God creates humanity in God's image to rule the birds and beasts and fish (v. 26), this is the kind of rule we should expect.

A rule like God's. A life-giving, gift-giving, empowering rule. The kind of rule that lets people see the sort of God who stands behind it. The kind of rule that flows from the God who shares power. The kind of rule that flows from the God who regains power through self-sacrifice at the cross.

In *The Lord of the Rings,* Gandalf issues a stern warning: "There is only one Lord of the Rings ... and he does not share power." Such have been all the life-sucking powers, great and small, that have taken their share of what they could grab hold of upon the earth. This is the way of sin and death in the story of the world as Paul tells it in Romans 5–8. But nothing could be farther from the God of Genesis 1 or of Romans 5.

In Romans 5, humanity's future is to rule in such a way that the self-giving Christ and son-giving God are put on full display. Empowering. Life-giving. Self-divesting. Renewed humanity, ruling in life through the one man, Jesus Christ. That's the vision of the future Paul puts before our eyes. Humanity restored.

When Paul says that "justification of life" comes through Jesus, this is what he means. The legal consequences of guilt are left behind and a new way of life, a new power, with a transformed future, becomes our reality.

The Power of Grace

In the final two verses of chapter 5, we learn that God's grace is more than a divine characteristic. It is one of the cosmic powers. Like sin. Like death. Except, not like them. Because it is greater.

In the presence of many transgressions, where the power of sin increased, the power of grace increased even more, strengthened by Jesus's one great life-bringing act. If sin is the instrument in the hands of death, strengthening the grip of its reign, then the righteous act of Jesus is the instrument in the hands of grace, which ushers humanity into eternal life.

Grace is the power of God, which takes hold of Jesus's faithful act—his death on the cross—and uses it to usher us through the final judgment and into the life to come. Into that place where we will reign. Into that place where we will know life as we have never known it before.

Or perhaps it is better to say … into that place where we will savor fully the life that we have only caught glimpses of here. It's the life that's found in the resurrection of Jesus. And we're about to find out that people who have been baptized into Jesus are no strangers to this existence.

CHAPTER SEVEN

Romans 6: Jesus: Where We Live & Move & Have our Being

Free from Sin—and Sinless?

At my alma mater, there is a large, bricked-in courtyard/square where students meet up before getting lunch or heading to the library. The university seems to have made it into a gathering spot in the hopes of diverting people's eyes from the horrific industrial 1960s monstrosities, constructed with utter contempt for the 1920s beauties carefully planned and executed a mere hundred yards away.

Let's just say that its name, "the Pit," is well earned.

During my time there, the Pit functioned as a sort of free speech zone. In this capacity, it regularly played host to traveling evangelists. We referred to these people as "Pit Preachers." Perhaps the most notorious pit preacher was Gary Birdsong. He would cast his accusatory message at the crowd with an opening salvo of, "Students, students, students." And out would come a litany of sins for which we needed to repent.

Sex and alcohol were at the top of his list. And Lord have mercy on women wearing shorts. (Side note: if Christianity exists to provide an alternative to sex and alcohol, then what faith is left for married people over the age of 21? And we wonder why youth group isn't a good pre-dictor of life-long church attendance...)

One of Birdsong's favorite arguments was that as a Christian, he no longer sinned. He would usually be met with derision for this one. Not a few of us reckoned that he had a few things to repent of just from his time in The Pit.

But he was armed with a verse from 1 John: "No one who remains in Him sins" (1 John 3:6). And he remained unmoved by the rebuttal of 1 John 1:8: "If we say we have no sin we deceive ourselves and the truth is not in us." Sometimes the Bible is complicated.

In my experience, the more common idea among Christians is that we all sin. A lot. Many churches feature a weekly prayer of confession in their public worship, acknowledging that we have done things we ought not to have, and that we have neglected to do things we ought to have done.

Some have gone even further. Martin Luther believed that the Christian life is so full of sin that Jesus's words "Repent, for the king-dom of God has come near" were meant to direct us toward an entire lifetime of repentance. This was the first of his famous Ninety-five Theses.

On the other hand, Jesus said a good tree will not bear bad fruit, nor a bad tree good fruit (Matthew 12:33–35). In this context, he was talking specifically about words. He seemed to expect at least a telling percentage of goodness from those who are good. And he assumed that the words of his opponents would be enough to condemn them when they stand before God.

So was Pit Preacher Birdsong closer to being correct than we gave him credit for?

In Romans 6–8, Paul describes what our life should look like if we've been swept up into the story he's telling. Remember that in Romans 5:12–21, Paul introduced the idea of sin as a ruling power. A power we will displace because of what Jesus did.

Paul is drawing lines between an old era of rule, initiated by Adam and typified by sin and death, and the new era of rule, initiated by Jesus and typified by grace, righteousness and life. Chapter 6 opens with a rhetorical question. In chapter 5, Paul had said that it's precisely where sin increased to a stranglehold that God's grace abounded most through the work of Jesus. Does this then mean that we should try to reenact the story in our own lives? Should we go on sinning, so that grace might increase (Romans 6:1)?

No way, says Paul. In fact, this question misses the whole story. It is in the one-off death of Jesus that the grace of God arrived to overcome the abundance of sin. We're not supposed to reenact that story by sinning and hoping for grace. We are to embody a different moment—the story's saving moment. The saving story becomes more and more ours as we live out our union with Jesus in his death and resurrection. We enter the story at the point of deliverance.

"In Christ"

It's time for a "here's something you need to know about how Paul thinks" moment. If you read through his letters, you'll find Paul saying stuff like "in Christ" or "with Christ" all over the place. Check out Ephesians 1 if you want to see his "in Christ" phraseology run amok. This is probably the single most important concept for understanding Paul's theory of salvation. To be saved is to be in a new place. It is "in Christ."

First, then, how do you get to this new place? Paul talks about it from different angles. The Spirit is important. So is the Lord's Supper. But according to Paul, baptism is the most crucial step to take in order to be "in Christ." Some years earlier, while writing to the Galatians, Paul stated, "All of you who were baptized into Christ have clothed yourselves with Christ" (Galatians 3:27). Here in Romans 6:3 he says, "All of us who were baptized into Christ were baptized into his death." Clearly, Paul assumes that baptism is the key mechanism for gaining unity with Christ.

This is not an easy concept. Do you remember those lines from *The Sound of Music*? You know, "How do you catch a cloud and pin it down?" and "How do you catch a wave upon the sand?" Sometimes trying to grasp union with Christ is a bit like that.

Generally speaking, it means that we take on Jesus's identity, and the things that are true about him become true of us as well. For instance, Jesus is God's son. Therefore, those who are in Christ are also sons and daughters of God (Galatians 3:26). More specifically, the saving narrative of Jesus's death and resurrection becomes the narrative of those who are united with him. Here, though, it's a bit tricky because Paul often urges us to make real in our own lives what is true about us in Christ.

That's why he'll say stuff like, "You've died with Christ—now, put to death the deeds of the flesh!" (Romans 8:13, paraphrased). And throughout 2 Corinthians, he presents his own suffering and hardship as proof that he is a legitimate minister of Jesus, that he is united to the crucified Christ.

One final aspect of union with Christ is important. It is not just about becoming a different kind of person—a "Christ person," if you will; it is also about the formation of a new people. Together. A new humanity for the new creation God is bringing about. There are multiple passages in the New Testament where Paul says things like, "There is no longer Jew or Greek, slave or free, male and female" (Galatians 3:28). This is a description of the new people that have been formed in Christ. And nearly the whole of Romans is taken up with explaining how he can possibly say that here, in Christ, there is no longer "Jew or Greek."

Sharing the Jesus Narrative

When Paul kicks things off in Romans 6, he assumes you know most of that. "Don't you know that all of us who were baptized into Christ Jesus (that's the shared assumption—everyone knows that baptism is "into Christ") were baptized into his death?" And that second part is what he wants us to learn. It's what he wants to build into his argument.

We share the Jesus narrative.

This is where the idea that sin and death are powers that would rule over humanity comes to the fore. As powers, they imposed a rule and a way of life. Jesus, through his death and resurrection, went through that rule and came out the other side to the rule of God and life and grace. Now we get to—*need* to—have Jesus's narrative become our own narrative as well.

The resurrection of Jesus energizes the life of those who are in Christ. For those of us still on this earth, resurrection is, ultimately, a hope for the future. But Romans 6 gives us the encouragement that we can take hold of that future and bring it to bear on the present.

We were baptized into his death and burial, so that as he was raised, we too, might now walk in newness of life (6:4). His story becomes our story. And crucially, "our" means more than "me, personally": we should be thinking about the new humanity Jesus represents. Don't let your translations fool you here. Some versions say that our old "self" was crucified with Christ (6:6). That's too individualistic. Paul says that our old "human" was crucified with Christ. He is continuing what he started in Romans 5:12–21, showing how humanity in Adam, with its subjugation to sin, death and corruption, is recreated as new humanity in Christ.

The resurrection shows that this old humanity has been done away with: "The One who died (i.e., Jesus) has been vindicated/justified from sin" (i.e., by his resurrection; 6:7). Again, various translations handle this differently. Many say something like, "Whoever dies has been freed from sin." But Paul's argument throughout Romans is that it's Jesus's death, not everyone's own death, that is the grounds for justification. The Greek literally says, "the one dying." Who is this referring to? Jesus fits the context best at this point. Based on Jesus's own movement from death to resurrection (which is Jesus's justification/vindication; 6:7), Paul invites us to live in accordance with who we are in Christ: we must live with Christ. That means not giving ourselves over to sin, but instead living under a new and better reign—the reign of life, the reign of God (6:8–11).

If you're looking for a short summary of Paul's argument in Romans 6, you'll find it in verses 12–14. Here, he concisely lays out the imperative for us to fully live out the Jesus story, while reminding us that sin no longer holds power over us. Don't let sin reign in your body, but instead present yourselves to God as people alive from the dead (6:12–13).

Speaking of Death

Paul wraps up the chapter by hammering away on the idea that sin's power leads to a life of slavery, which leads to death.

Pause.

We need to talk about "death" for a second. When we read the Bible, most of us tend to mush together all the different writers and their theologies. But not all biblical writers have the same ideas about everything, including what might happen to a person if they don't accept the gospel story.

Remember that Paul's whole understanding of salvation is wrapped up in the story of Jesus's death and resurrection. Salvation is union with him. The reason there is hope for life beyond death is that Jesus has been raised from the dead. Why can we have hope for eternal life? Because we have been united to Jesus who has already entered his, by his resurrection.

If future, eternal life is dependent on being joined to Jesus, where does that leave people who have *not* been joined? It leaves them, simply, dead. Both physically and spiritually dead. While Paul might imagine the departed standing before God for final judgment, any condemnation he envisions would simply leave them without access to the positive good of life in Jesus. Paul does not have an idea of hell, because hell would require a resurrected body—and resurrection is only found in Christ.

So when Paul says that the wages of sin is death (6:23), he is talking about the same kind of death Jesus endured: a body that does not function. He has no notion of a spirit that lives separate from it. When Paul speaks later of condemnation (e.g., Romans 8:1), he likely imagines being condemned to this fate: a dead body that is not raised.

Different New Testament writers have other ways of depicting life for the condemned on the other side of the final judgment, but Paul is likely what modern theologians would call an "annihilationist": anyone condemned simply ceases to exist. Here, as in several other important areas, by binding the books of the New Testament under one cover we have permanently enshrined theological diversity into the story of the church.

What this means for us, in part, is that the work Paul is trying to do in Romans—the work of getting a theologically, ethnically, and even ethically diverse people to worship God together under the lordship of Jesus—is work that will always be with us. Theological diversity is an inherent part of Christianity: a feature rather than a bug. One place where we need to cultivate comfort with diversity is in people's views of the End. Especially because, if what happened with the arrival of Jesus is any indication, the climactic actions of God will no doubt surprise us all.

Unpause.

Okay, so here we are at the end of Romans 6, where Paul is hammering away at how the power of sin makes us slaves.

> "You're slaves of the one whom you obey ..." (6:16).
> "You were slaves of sin ..." (6:17).
> "You presented the parts of your bodies to be slaves of impurity and lawlessness ..." (6:19).
> "You were slaves of sin ... bearing fruit for death" (6:20–21).
> "The wages of sin is death..." (6:23).

Okay, so it's probably not fair to say that Paul wraps up the chapter just hammering away about how bad sin is. Because throughout these verses, he's contrasting, cajoling and inviting the Romans to recognize the path of freedom that God has offered.

> "You can be slaves of sin, *or* … of obedience leading to righteousness" (6:16).
> "You were slaves, *but* you became obedient from the heart …" (6:17).
> "You used to present your bodies to be slaves of impurity … *now* you have presented your bodies to serve purity and righteousness" (6:19).
> "Freed from sin, having been made servants to God, you bear the fruit of eternal life" (6:22).
> "The wages of sin is death, *but* the gift of God is eternal life …" (6:23).

All this contrasting of slavery to sin and "slavery" to righteousness (I use scare quotes because Paul tells us in verse 19 that he's using a figure of speech to try to penetrate their thick skulls) is ultimately to show that faithful obedience to God is an inherent part of the story he is inviting both Jews and Gentiles into.

So What About the Law?

The question looming over all of verses 16–23 is this: "Shall we sin because we are not under law but under grace?" The Reformation helped cement an interpretation of this question that generalizes "law" to "doing stuff" (or "works"). But remember that Paul is talking about Jewish, biblical law-keeping, specifically. And when he uses phrases like "under law" and "under grace" he is referring to the powers that reign. The nub of his argument is this: uncoupling the Jewish law from the identity of God does not create a people who will sin; instead, it creates a people who are uniquely able to faithfully serve God.

According to the argument Paul makes, divorcing the law from the identity of the people of God does not make morality optional or unlikely. It makes a life that is approved by God possible in a way that it was not before. Many of the things we hope to see from those who are in Christ match what was expected of Israel (see Romans 13), but there are some profound changes as well (see Romans 14–15).

The extensive contrast between slavery to sin and the freedom that God offers is Paul's argument in favor of grace. Something has changed. Something profound. We have a new master. The short confession "Jesus is Lord" tells us that God's rule has been reestablished upon the earth. We might say the Kingdom of God has come near. It required the dethroning of the ones who ruled when he arrived. Sin and death.

This ability to conquer sin and death is exactly what the law was never able to do. That is why law was not the answer to humanity's problem. Which also means, for Paul, that people who want to be part of the family of God do not have to be "in the law" to be justified. They have to be "in Christ." He opens the way for what the law promised but could not deliver: faithful obedience to God leading to justification.

The End has Begun, but …

The life completely without sin, the life that has conquered death, is one of the promises in Paul's story. But the fact that it comes through the resurrection is a double-edged sword. Because Jesus's resurrection has taken place, but ours has not. Resurrection is the lynchpin of what nerds call "eschatology": what is going to happen at the End. The End: with a final judgment that ensures justice in the world, a new creation that displays God's final victory over the forces of decay and death, people raised from the dead to inhabit this world in glorified bodies, a global and multilingual people that show for all eternity that God is the God of all.

We need this multifaceted picture of the End to fully grasp the importance of Jesus's resurrection. Because Jesus has been raised, the

End has already begun. In fact, Jesus's resurrection is the first verdict that God has cast at the Last Judgment. But if this is all we say, then we'll misstep badly. Theology that stops with the arrival of the last days is guilty of what nerds call "over-realized eschatology." It reads too much of the future into the present.

Because the world continues to be full of sin and death, the End has not fully arrived.

The new creation has begun, but it is the sequel to a story that has not yet fully resolved. This is why Paul says that Jesus has overcome the power of sin in his resurrection, while simultaneously enjoining us to make the power of righteousness real in our own lives. The End is here, but the transition is not complete.

So where does that leave the perfect, sinless Pit Preacher?

I would say he is imagining himself to be living further in the future than he actually is. (See my comments on "over-realized eschatology.") He's not sinless yet, because he is still in a body that will succumb to the reign of death.

And where does all this leave Martin Luther, with his whole life of repentance? I would say Luther and his followers imagine themselves to be living in a world with less of a presence of Jesus's resurrection life than Paul proclaims. Nerds call this "under-realized eschatology."

Luther needed to bring more of the future into the present. The end truly has begun. The death knell of sin's reign has been rung. Jesus is Lord. It is possible to shift allegiance. That's the whole point. It is actually possible to obey God, and not simply become more aware of how far short we have fallen.

To put another nerd-term on it, we are living in a time of "inaugurated eschatology." The End has begun, but the prior word is still being spoken. The imposter king has been defeated, but he is still fighting for the throne. The power of the resurrection is, in fact, present here and now, but we are also still looking forward to the resurrection of our bodies. The new creation has begun to dawn, but our bodies and the world around us are still subject to corruption, death and decay. Jesus is Lord, but idolatry still pulls us away in service of other masters.

Walking into the Gift

Paul concludes Romans 6 with one of his best-known verses: "The wages of sin is death, but the gift of God is eternal life in Christ Jesus our Lord" (6:23). When reading this verse, it's easy to miss the fact that this promise of the "gift" of eternal life comes at the end of a chapter dedicated to telling us that we can, in fact, obey God. It comes at the end of a paragraph whose whole purpose is to demonstrate that freedom from sin means service to God.

Check out those lists above. Eternal life is the fruit of a life lived in righteous service. So the "gift" here isn't out of the blue. The "gift" of eternal life does not ignore what we do with our lives. The gift of eternal life begins with the cross. It finds its life-giving power in the resurrection: the vindication that brings new life. The gift takes root in us as it unites us to Christ. It grows in us as our lives better retell his story—putting to death the deeds of the body, presenting our members as instruments of righteousness to God. The gift is living under God's reign rather than under the reign of sin and death.

So when the gift brings us final, eschatological life, it is not out of the blue. It is not without regard to the lives we have lived. It is confirmation of what we have been becoming. It's an ending that fits. It is a resurrection life for those who have learned what it is to be crucified with Christ.

CHAPTER EIGHT

Romans 7: Legal Troubles

When Laws are Weird

I grew up in a Navy family. My dad enlisted in college and retired the same year I graduated from high school. One of the markers of military family life is the specter of moving every two to three years. With this came various dreams and fears of where we might end up. We dreamed of Panama and ended up in Spain. While in Spain we dreamed of Singapore.

In the days before the internet, moving someplace completely unknown was even more mysterious. And terrifying. For a middle-school boy, the excitement of relocating to Singapore was colored by some pretty stark fears. Because laws.

Now that the internet exists, I wanted to see if what I remembered was simply misremembered facts. Or maybe I had been told urban legends that were not actually true. But no. There is a real live article on the internet (hence, Truth) entitled, "10 weird laws in Singapore that could get you in trouble." I'm serious. She didn't use any capital letters in her blog post title. Terrifying. But I digress ...

Among these ten "weird laws" are the two that I remembered.

No spitting.

No gum.

I've never been much of an expectorator. But I had visions of for-getting one day or of having an uncontrollable need to spit and winding up in jail in a foreign country where I didn't speak the language, my innocence gone, falling into a life of crime at the age of fourteen. As it turns out, we ended up in Northern Virginia, an experience that made a jail in Singapore start to sound pretty good. But that's another story.

Living abroad can help you realize that laws, as often as not, are expres-sions of particular cultures. They enshrine local values more than they reflect "universal" norms.

Those of us who live in the US don't even need to leave our home country to find this out. You can get a taste of it by living abroad in San Francisco or Texas without even having to get a passport! (Yet.)

Here's the important thing: whenever we're inside a system, the laws seem normal. Go someplace else and they seem "weird." Leaving behind what is familiar can be discomforting. That all gets ticked up a notch when the laws and standards are wedded to religious beliefs.

Laws people believe have come from God are even more difficult to interrogate, let alone relinquish. If we truly believe that a law, or a system of laws, is of God, then we're also likely to believe that no one is on God's side unless they reside fully within that legal framework. By definition, those who refuse to abide by that framework do not—cannot—belong to the people of God. Moreover, if God has given the laws, then the people who see and acknowledge and keep those laws, the people who build their lives around honoring what God has said, can surely anticipate that God will honor, bless and, in the end, vindi-cate them and their way of life.

So here comes Paul—the first-century equivalent of an American expat who informs Singaporeans that tobacco spitting and gum chewing now are acceptable practices in their country. In fact, they're where Singapore has been headed all along!

He's brought Gentiles to the Jewish God, but in the process, he's also made the argument that Jewish identity as the people of God does not depend on them keeping the law of Moses. In fact, he argues that the law is a hindrance. An obstacle. An omen of death rather than the harbinger of life that God had promised it would be.

So how on earth can Paul hold onto his deeply biblical, Jewish sensibility that the law is a good thing, given by God, while simultaneously claiming that it is now basically irrelevant for defining what faithfulness to God looks like? It's overstating things to say that in jumping from Adam to Christ, Paul has written the law out of God's saving story. But he has definitely stripped it of its leading role. And he stands in danger of recasting it as the enemy of God's people.

When the Law Defines a Relationship

So as you work your way through Romans 7, remember that Paul is trying to thread the needle between the law being a good gift from God, and the law being unnecessary for salvation or defining the people of God. This also means that he is not creating a generalized juxtaposition between doing things versus trusting God—which is what modern Christians often think is going on when Paul talks about faith versus works.

His concern is much more specific. This is about the place of the law of Moses (those particular works) in relation to the death and resurrection of Jesus (that specific faith).

Romans 7 is divided into three sections. In the first section, Paul uses the analogy of marriage to show why we are no longer bound to the law (7:1–6). Then Paul realizes he might have backed himself into a corner, so he asks (basically, in his best Jim Carey voice), "Alrighty then, does this mean the law is sin?" and spends the next section finding ways to say no (7:7–13). The last part of the chapter is the one you've probably heard of. Paul goes around and around saying that he doesn't do what he wants to do but does the very thing he doesn't want (7:14–25). Spoiler alert: this last paragraph of Romans 7 probably doesn't mean what you think it does. So stick around for that.

Paul uses the analogy of marriage to show that laws have their limits. Marriage laws create legal expectations—but only while one of the partners is alive. Therefore, one cannot commit adultery against a deceased spouse. In fact, you're now free to be joined with someone else! Paul really has romantic notions of marriage, am I right?

The analogy is just to make a point. He articulates it like this: We (probably Jews) died to the law through Christ's body, so that we could be joined to another—the resurrected Jesus (7:4). Don't look too closely at this one; you'll hurt your eyes trying to bring the whole thing into focus.

Basically, Paul is saying that the law governed humanity as it was in Adam: enslaved to the powers of sin and death. Jesus came in "the likeness of sinful flesh" (see Romans 8:3), which means he was joined with all of humanity under the law's jurisdiction. And he died. Since we are joined to Jesus (we are "in Christ"), his death frees us from being bound up with sinful, Adam-condemned humanity. Like Jesus—in Jesus—we are freed from the reign of sin or the governance of the law.

Not only are we released from the old beau, but we also have a new and better one. The resurrected Jesus, not under the law, not under the sway of sin and death, offers us, in himself, a new humanity to be wed to. With a new partner we get a new life—no more bearing fruit for death. "We serve in newness of the Spirit, not in oldness of the letter" (Romans 7:6). Remember that it's the Spirit who raised Jesus (Romans 1:4). We share in Jesus's resurrection life. Jesus, by the Spirit, not the law, is what makes God-honoring service possible.

In Bad Company

What Paul says about the law puts it in some bad company. In that first stage of life, while "we" were "in the flesh," the law caused sinful desires to arise. This "bore fruit" in death (Romans 7:5). In chapters 5 and 6, Paul talked about the power of sin and death. Now, he aligns them with the law. Far from being part of God's rescue plan, the law does the opposite of what it was intended to do. It makes sin worse. Stronger. More pervasive. And it cements sin's wages by leading to death.

Paul's aligning of sin and death with the law is pervasive. In the few verses of the marriage analogy and its explanation, Paul repeatedly deploys words and images to talk about the law that he initially used in chapter 6 to talk about sin. Not all the examples translate exactly from Greek to English, but here's what I'm talking about:

- In 6:6, the body of sin is "released" or "abolished" (Greek, *katargēthē*). In 7:2 and 7:6, one is "released" (*katērgētai, katērgēthēmen*) from the law.
- In 6:6, people are "slaves" (*douleuein*) to sin. In 7:6, people were "slaves" (*douleuein*) in the oldness of the Letter (of the law).
- In 6:9, death was "lord" (*kurieuei*). In 6:14, sin was "lord" (*kurieusei*). In 7:1, the law is "lord" (*kurieuei*) until someone dies.
- In 6:10–11, Christ and his believers "die" (*apethanen*) to sin. In 7:4, they "die" (*ethanatōthēte*) to the law.
- In 6:18, 6:20 and 6:22, the work of Christ is to "free" (*eleutherōthentes, eleutheroi*) people from sin. In 7:3, one is "free" (*eleuthera*) from the law.
- In 6:20–21, the life before Christ is seen as having "fruit" (*karpon*, 6:21), through sin, that ends in death. In 7:5, the law arouses sinful passions, which bear the "fruit" (*karpophorēsai*) of death.

Paul has systematically redeployed the language he previously used to talk about sin to talk about the law. Now do you see why, coming to the end of the marriage analogy, Paul says, "What am I saying? That the law is sin?" Well, Paul, it sure looks like it.

Wielded by Sin

The next section (Romans 7:7–13) is fairly easy to summarize. The law isn't sin—it's holy, righteous and good. But ... it gets taken advantage of by sin. Sin takes hold of the law like it's a weapon, using it to kill people. That's how you know how bad sin is: it can take hold of something good and make something terrible happen.

But there are a couple of fascinating turns in the argument that deserve our attention. Perhaps the most pervasive theme in the whole of Romans is that the resurrection of Jesus shows that God has done in Christ what the law was never able to do: bring life to humanity. But this does not mean the law was entirely without life-giving power. "When the commandment came, sin became alive, and I died" (7:9). The word that Paul uses for "became alive" is often used to describe "resurrection" elsewhere in the New Testament. Here, then, is the law's life-giving power—it gives life to sin and death!

This, by the way, is the complete opposite of what the law says about itself (see Deuteronomy 30:15–16). But because of the death and resurrection of Jesus, Paul finds himself needing to tell a different story. A story in which the law does not play a saving role. A story in which resurrection life comes from Jesus paying the law's penalty, not from Jesus fulfilling the law's every command. Throughout his letters Paul is rewriting the story, struggling to give the law its proper place. Something holy, righteous and good in itself (Romans 7:12), and yet implicated in the reign of sin and death.

In short, the law lacked the power to make us the kind of people who could lead lives pleasing to God. It could not make us spiritual. That's what Paul wrestles with in the last section of this chapter.

Doing and Not Doing When "I" Know Better

In what would become some of his most instantly recognizable words, in Romans 7:14–25 Paul articulates being stuck between knowing the right things to do and the inexorable pull of doing just the opposite.

"The things I do, I don't understand, because I don't do the things that I want to do. But the things I don't wish to do? Yeah, I do those." Who hasn't felt that at some point in their lives? It's like there's some power deep inside of us. Sabotaging us. Paul names that power "sin."

That's what's to blame for this dissonance. Sin is the indwelling power, the reason we do the things we shouldn't (7:17, 7:20 and 7:23).

One reason this paragraph is difficult to pin down is that it assumes the character of speech. Paul has actually been doing this a lot in Romans; so when he says "I," it does not necessarily mean him in the present. It could be him in the past. Or it could be that he's taking on the position of a Jew living under the law. Or it could be that he is using "I" as a stand-in for the whole people of Israel. Or it could be humanity, as a whole, in Adam. Scholars have argued for each of these positions.

The way Paul opens and closes this section of his argument suggests he is not speaking of himself in his present life "in Christ." He begins by saying, "We know that the law is spiritual, but I am of flesh, sold into slavery to sin" (7:14). The whole point of the previous two chapters has been to show that people who are in Christ, joined to his death and resurrection, are no longer slaves to sin. People can share in a new reign, serve a new master.

Moreover, on several occasions Paul has reiterated that the Spirit is part of God's gift that leads to life. Having the Spirit, or being a "Spiritual" person, is the opposite of being "in the flesh" as Paul uses those ideas. So whatever character Paul is taking on in this section, it's not the voice of someone who is living the life of faith.

At the conclusion of the section, Paul asks, "Who will set me free from this body of death?" And he has an answer: "Thanks be to God through Jesus Christ our Lord" (7:24–25). The gospel Paul has been proclaiming contains the resolution to the conflict between knowing what is right and actually doing it. Those who are in Christ already have this deliverance. They are free.

What I'm saying is this: as much as this passage has resonated with Christians down through the centuries as a picture of their own life struggles as people of faith, that is likely not what Paul is trying to portray.

The portrait here is much closer to the lawless Gentile of Romans 1: someone who knows what God would have him do, but is handed over, almost against his will, to the things he knows are wrong. There is a difference, though, in that the character to whom Paul is giving voice in chapter 7 delights in the law and truly wants to keep it. But he can't.

This suggests that Paul is speaking, perhaps obliquely, about the life of Israel outside of Christ. Either his own experience before he was called by Jesus, or a personification of the struggles of Israel—a nation that, despite its reverence for the law, repeatedly comes under God's judgment for failing to keep it. Of these two options, Paul's indications that his life in Judaism, under the law, was not conflicted, but very much successful and righteous (Philippians 3:6), suggest that he has the turbulent history of Israel in mind in Romans 7.

Reflecting on Discomfiting Biblical Interpretation

The deeply conflicted ego of Romans 7:14–25 has been a mainstay for many followers of Jesus. Paul's plaintive cry, "Wretched man that I am, who will set me free?" no doubt inspired John Newton as he penned, "Amazing grace, how sweet the sound that saved a wretch like me."

I wonder if any feelings come up for you when I say that Paul is not talking about the Christian life here, but instead a conflict that being in Christ should fully resolve. Does any of this get at what you're experiencing?

Do you just roll your eyes at the smarty-pants bible nerd who thinks he can take away from an important experience or scripture passage?

Do you feel disoriented about your own life looking really different from what Paul seems to expect?

Is there anxiety at the idea of having heard so many people possibly misinterpret a passage of scripture?

Are you annoyed at my obvious inability to read the plain words on the page?

Do me a favor and sit with those questions for a minute.

And even if you don't personally resonate with any of these responses, can you imagine what it's like to be someone who does?

After you've gotten yourself into that mindset and you've recognized the difficult emotions that can arise when someone "takes away" a favorite Bible passage, imagine that you're a first-century Jew.

You're listening to Paul. And he has the gall to tell you that every Bible passage you've built your whole life on needs to be read differently. And the law that God gave, which has been such a comfort to you, is being held up as a source of sin and death instead of life and salvation.

It has to feel like he's taking away everything. Because in a sense, he is. Paul is transforming and changing everything about every Bible verse you've known and loved and built your life on. But while he's doing that, he's telling you that this is what you were holding onto all along, the true ending of the story of the law.

This is not bringing a few tobacco-spitting Americans and their disrespectful, bubble gum–blowing kids to Singapore. This is airdropping wads of chewed-up gum onto the streets and installing spittoons on every corner, then calling it all "True Singapore."

In some ways, it's much easier to claim that Jesus brings in a new humanity than to articulate how he creates a new people. Because "new humanity" can remain vague. Ephemeral. But a "new people" will be a new tribe with new boundaries and new rules. Or, at least, it will flout the old boundaries and the old rules.

And when those old rules have been given by God, literally written in stone … well, let's just say that it's going to take a lot of work to reimagine what God might want instead. And it will take a lot to convince someone that the work should be done. That the old should be given up in favor of the new. It will take a miracle.

For Paul, it takes a resurrection.

CHAPTER NINE

Romans 8: Resurrection People

Transformation

Do you want to start with the good news or the bad news?

Oh my gosh, Kirk, Romans 8 is like the most explosively amazing chapter in the whole Bible and you're bringing bad news into this? Really? #Enneagram8

Okay, you make a good point. I apologize. Let's start with the good news.

Romans 8 is about transformation. It is from start to finish about being transformed from the inside out. Just think about how much time and energy we devote to becoming the best versions of ourselves. Or to creating the best versions of our communities, businesses or families.

- Taking personality tests.
- Seeking professional coaching.
- Finding mentorship.
- Participating in work evaluations and reviews.
- Attending therapy.

- Volunteering.
- Praying.
- Meditating.
- Attending worship services.
- Reading books by experts.
- Listening to podcasts.
- Going on retreats.

Personal transformation, taken altogether, is a behemoth, diverse industry. That's capitalism's way of saying it is very, very important. And Romans 8 is all about transformation. It's about becoming single-minded. It's about living into what we know is good and right. Romans 8 is the answer to the conflict so many of us resonate with in Romans 7: How do we break free from that trap of not doing what we want to do and instead doing the very things we hate?

This climactic chapter answers this question in a sweeping, all-encompassing way. It reaches into the depths of our inner world, wraps up our everyday activities and does not stop until it has us located in a family that can facilitate this growth, located on a planet renewed to sustain us while we care for it.

It's all right here. It's literally everything.

In the face of this, what bad news could there possibly be?! Good question. You might want to sit down. You ready? Here goes.

There are no imperatives. There are no instructions. The chapter does not give us anything to do.

It is a description of the all-encompassing transformation that God gives through the Spirit who raised Jesus from the dead. It is a declaration of all things being made new. But frustratingly, agonizingly, infuriatingly … it doesn't give us anything to do.

It's a portrait of grace. A picture that should be a mirror. So we can gaze at it. And hope that its hues become our own. We can get lost in it. And find ourselves with Paul, carried away in praise of what we see.

Christ "for" Us? Or Us "in" Christ? Yes.

Historically, Paul's interpreters have struggled with how to hold together the two different ways in which he talks about the work of Jesus. On the one hand, there is what Christ does *for* other people. Christ died "for me." On the other hand, there is what Christ does *in solidarity with* people. Christ "in me," or me "in Christ."

The first is most closely tied with justification and forgiveness of sins. It deals with sin as guilt. The second is most commonly associated with being transformed, becoming a new person. It deals with sin as power.

I can imagine Paul responding to this difficulty in the tender words of my blessed teenage children: "Sounds like a you problem."

Because it's not a problem that Paul has himself. Romans 8 begins with a triumphant declaration: "There is now no *condemnation* for those who are *in Christ Jesus*" because God's Spirit of life has set people *free* (8:1–2). Death is overcome: we both come through the final judgment and find ourselves receiving the gift of Christ's own resurrection life. Being in Christ, freed from sin's power: these are the reasons why justification and forgiveness happen.

And there's another reason. Because God did in Christ what the law could never do. God condemned all of sin in Jesus, who bore the likeness of sinful flesh (8:3). This means that there is a new opportunity. A chance at true life. It comes from the transforming work of the Spirit (8:4–11).

In Paul's mind, there is no disjunction between Jesus dying on the cross for our sins and people receiving new life from the Spirit who raised Jesus from the dead. Together, these holy actions created a new standing before God: people are now able to walk in ways that are pleasing to God.

The transformation that consumes Paul's vision is available to everyone who has the Spirit: "You are no longer in 'the flesh' but in the Spirit—if the Spirit of God lives in you" (8:9). Good thing, too.

Because being in "the flesh" means that you can't please God (8:8).
It's that whole Romans 7 thing about not being able to do what's right.
In Romans 8, we learn that the flesh has been overcome.

Flesh and Body

So what about this talk of "the flesh"? Does that mean the body is bad?
Basically, yes. But that's not the end of the story.

Paul definitely displays an ancient hierarchical worldview, which
values the inner person as the place of strength and reason, through
which a righteous person might win out against the inferior body with
its yearning desires. But "flesh" and "body" aren't identical. And one of
the great transformations that happens with the freedom Christ brings
is that our "members" (as he puts it in chapter 6), which is to say "the
parts of our body," can be presented to God for service.

More importantly, Jesus was raised from the dead. To be raised
from the dead means that a person has a body again, a transformed
body fit for the Spirit and new creation.

This is the life-giving power of the Spirit that Paul envisions dwell-
ing in those who are in Christ. This means that while still inhabiting
a fleshy body, the "spiritual mind" can win out. We are no longer "in
the flesh," no longer in the realm where the flesh is subjected to sin and
death. Instead, we are "in the Spirit," in the realm where the Spirit and
life and righteousness hold sway.

And, finally (I mean really and truly finally, as in "the End," when
God judges the world and everyone gets what's coming to them), "God
who raised Jesus will also give life to your mortal body through God's
Spirit" (8:11). Bodies aren't inherently bad. They are redeemable. They
are not necessarily portals of sin's power. They can be subjected to the
life-giving power of the Spirit.

In all this, don't miss how critical the resurrection of Jesus is. Remember Paul's cry in chapter 7: "Who will set me free from this body of

death?" The answer, given in chapter 8, is that deliverance from death is resurrection.

The Spirit in Romans is defined as the Spirit who raised Jesus from the dead (Romans 1:4). That is its identity. The One who enables a new way of life. That is the One who brings the transformation we struggle to work out on our own because the desires of the flesh (bodies, yes, but more: bodies and brains enslaved to sin and death) overwhelm the desires of the mind.

Son of God / Children of God

There's something else Paul says about the Spirit and resurrection in chapter 1 that is critical here in chapter 8. Romans 1:4 says that Jesus "was appointed Son of God with power by the resurrection from the dead." In Paul's understanding, the resurrection is transformative for who Jesus is. Like the Davidic kings "become" God's sons when they were enthroned (see Psalm 2), Jesus "becomes" God's son when he is raised and enthroned as Spirit-transformed Lord.

If you read the Gospels, you can see a similar theology applied earlier in Jesus's life. In Mark, which has no birth narrative, the first time we see Jesus is at his baptism, where he receives the Spirit and God declares him to be God's Son (Mark 1:11; this passage is also tied to the crucifixion, but that's another story). In Luke, which *does* have a birth story, the connection gets pushed back even further, to his conception, when the angel says that Jesus will be conceived by the Spirit and that is why he will be called God's Son (Luke 1:35).

The point—though the timing might differ (again ... that's a whole other book!)—the consistent point across all accounts is that Jesus's sonship is inseparable from his being marked by the Spirit. Jesus's Spiritual sonship comes first and ours follows.

This is the lynchpin for getting our heads around what Paul says about us. "All who are being led by the Spirit of God—these are children (literally, "sons") of God" (8:14). Later Paul will say that Jesus is the firstborn among many siblings (8:29).

Our place in the family is derived from his. To be in Christ is to be in the Spirit, part of the family of God. This is what it looks like to be rescued from life in Adam, which is life in the flesh.

There is no one way to explain this. How are we God's new-creation family? It is because the Spirit that confers Jesus's sonship is also in us. It is because we are in Christ, so that what is true of him is true of us. It is because God is transforming us into what humanity was always supposed to be, which Christ already is. It is because of the Spirit. It is because of Jesus. It is because of us.

All of this is bound up in the story of Jesus. To have the Spirit is to be God's heir. This also means we find ourselves on the journey of suffering with Christ in order to be finally glorified with him (8:17). We move with him from death to resurrection. Romans 8 depicts human transformation as the embodiment of the Jesus story.

What's Coming Is What Happened to Jesus

In the second half of the chapter, Paul looks further into the future, to the things we hope for but don't yet experience (Romans 8:18–39). This is the transformation that we will never fully see in this life.

Throughout the scriptures of Israel there is a connection between God's chosen human representatives and the land on which they live. The land mirrors the health of the people's relationship with God, with each other and with the nations. When the people neglect their obligations, the land suffers. When justice and righteousness flow through the people, abundance flows through the land. So of course, when all things are finally renewed, the wolf will live with the lamb, the leopard will lie down with the goat (in peace … not to eat them for dinner; Isaiah 11:6).

So if this story is to find itself put back together again, if the law and the prophets bear witness to the crucified and risen Christ, then restoration cannot stop with humans. And it certainly could not have its ending with humans floating off to heaven to be with God in the sky forever. This biblical narrative can only be concluded where it started: with all of creation rightly ordered, flourishing, thriving, being fruitful and multiplying, as God originally intended. And with, at long last, a faithful humanity embodying the truth of God's own presence upon its land.

This is what Paul hopes for (8:19–23). He anticipates that our future—new life, freedom, wholeness, joy—will wrap up the whole of creation and bring it into a place of new life. He hopes that even as Jesus's move from suffering to glory sets us free, if only in some incipient way, so too our move from suffering to glory will set all of creation free.

Creation was subjected to futility because of human choice and action (8:20). It will be set free for glory because of human redemption and restoration (8:21). As we receive new life, and restoration to our status as God's children, through the resurrection life of Jesus, so too will the creation be restored with the resurrection of our own bodies (8:23).

I started this chapter with a good news, bad news scenario: Romans 8 is all about transformation but gives no instructions on how to accomplish it. I think Paul might have felt the weight of this. Because as he approaches the climax of this chapter, which is the climax of the letter so far, he places the whole thing in the hands of God.

We don't know. We don't know what to do. We don't even know what to say. We don't know how to pray. But the Spirit takes care of that, interceding on our behalf with wordless groans (8:26). And the God whose reign extends over all space and time ensures that those prayers are heard. God causes all things to work together for good for those who love God (8:28).

God holds together the past, present and future as if they are already completed actions (we are foreknown, set apart, called, justified, glorified; 8:29–30). God knows people before they even know themselves. And God sets them aside for a purpose. For *The* Purpose.

The purpose of being restored to the fullness of what it means to be truly human. Which is to say, to be transformed into the image of Jesus (8:29). Just as we were truly human in the beginning, when humanity was created in the image of God.

Romans 1:4 tells us that Jesus was "set aside" (Greek: *horizo*) as God's son by the Spirit raising him from the dead. Here, Paul puts a prefix on that verb to say that God "set aside beforehand" (*prohorizo*) people to become conformed to the Son's image. God had decided to make a new family. The reason Paul makes a point of it is to express his confidence that God's got hold of us: God is going to ensure that God's people know the fullness of new life in Christ in the restored new creation. We're going to see in the next chapter that Paul's thoughts have not strayed far from the troubling question of the Jews' rejection of Jesus as messiah. He is, in part, setting us up to understand that God has a future for Israel.

But for now, Paul's focus is on the fact that Jesus is the firstborn from the dead. And we are the family of those reborn from the dead. He is our older brother. We are his sisters and brothers. The children of God. We share in the resurrection life of Jesus. Set apart as he was. Called as he was. Justified as he was. Glorified as he was.

God. It's About God.

The ultimate trust in the future God has for us is that all these things are from God. "If God is for us, who could be against us?" (8:31). Grounding this hope is the one great, sacrificial action of God. "He did not spare his own son but delivered him up for us all" (8:32).

The language Paul uses here, "did not spare his own son," evokes and echoes the words that God spoke to Abraham after the near-sacrifice of Isaac. Because Abraham "does not spare" his son Isaac, God affirms that Abraham's descendants would be as numerous as the stars of the sky. Moreover, because of Abraham's obedience, his descendants would bring blessing on the nations of the earth (Genesis 22:16–18).

So even here, when Paul is casting our gaze to the cosmic throne room of God, where he imagines no criminal charge being able to stand against us, no enemy power able to prevail, he is continuing to reframe what it means to be the people of God, the children of Abraham. Abraham did not spare his son—but God did. In contrast, God did not spare God's own son; the knife, so to speak, was not stayed. The promise to Abraham finds its fulfillment in God's later work. The greater Abraham. And the nations are entering the blessing.

What blessing? The blessing of being given everything—the whole cosmos—as we share in what God gives to Jesus (8:32).

What is the source of hope? God. Remember that the larger question that stands over the issue of Israel's faithfulness is God's own faithfulness. Can God be trusted? What does it mean to have God in charge of this particular story with its surprising twists and turns? Will this story reach its promised climax in the vindication of God's people? Here is Paul's answer: God is the justifier—and we've already been justified. Who could condemn (8:33)?

Oh yeah, and the work of Jesus that brought justification onto the cosmic stage? That movement from death to resurrection? It sits, embodied in Jesus's own person, at God's right hand (8:34). The reminder, the whisper if necessary, that everything has been taken care of. Here, in Jesus, is the embodiment of a life right with God. It's a life in which we have all been included.

With God as the insurance for glory in the age to come, and with Jesus as our own embodied future at God's right hand, the future is not in doubt. All potential enemies are mocked. The love of Christ, the love of God, triumphs in the end.

Who, or what, could ever separate us from the love of Christ? Tribulation or calamity or persecution or famine or nakedness or danger or sword? ... In all these things we are the great conquerors through him who loved us. For I am persuaded that neither death nor life, neither angels nor cosmic powers, neither things present

nor things to come nor powers, neither height nor depth nor anything else in all the created world, will be able to separate us from
the love of God that is in Christ Jesus our Lord. (8:35–39)

Great, conquering hope. Grounded in love. Beginning with the love of
Christ (Paul gives one of his very rare statements about Jesus's love for
us in 8:35) and culminating with the love of God (8:39).

The victory of God over the powers that array themselves against
God's world is the victory of love. Victory over the powers of sin and
death is the victory of the love of Jesus, who endured sin and death in
order to be freed from them by the power of the Spirit.

The gospel story of Jesus tells the story of our future. Vindication.
Victory. Life. A family. A new creation.

The love of God in Christ Jesus our Lord.

CHAPTER TEN

So, About the Cross

On Being a PEACH

I hang out with a bunch of PEACHes. Those would be Post-Evangelical Agnostic Christian Humanists. Let me flesh this out for you real quick.

Post-Evangelical: someone whose understanding of Christianity is shaped by an evangelical upbringing, but who no longer identifies with that tribe for whatever reason.

Agnostic: someone who is not entirely sure what exactly is true concerning God and the stories we tell about God.

Christian: someone whose understanding of what goodness looks like in this world is shaped by the story of Jesus. Teachings like "Love your neighbor as yourself" and "Do unto others as you would have them do unto you" rank high with these folks.

Humanist: I'm misappropriating this term, using it to refer to someone who believes that whatever a person's faith—or politics—looks like, it should be good for actual people. If your theology makes you a jerk, then it's bad theology.

In summary, don't be a jerk. Be a PEACH. Love Jesus. Love the person next to you.

I mention all this because these people, my tribe, such as it is, do a lot of thinking about the cross. What does it mean? Why did it have to happen? What does it say about God? What does it say about us that we would worship a God who would place a torture device at the center of their religion?

Throughout Romans 1–8 we have seen (and somewhat skirted around) Paul giving answers to these questions. Answers that sound a lot like the answers many of us were given in church growing up. Answers we don't like. Answers we have good theological reasons for not giving anymore. But they are Paul's answers—biblical answers—nonetheless.

For instance: does God require Jesus's death in order to forgive sins? Can people be declared "not guilty" without Jesus dying? There are other mechanisms for forgiving sins in the Bible. Even in the New Testament. John the Baptist forgives people's sins through baptism (Mark 1:4). Jesus forgives sins with a word of authority, given to him from God (Mark 2:5–12).

But Paul does not tell stories of Jesus's life from before the cross. Neither does Paul claim that some external principle compels God to wait for Jesus's death before extending true, eternal forgiveness.

Paul does not begin with a set of prerequisites generated by the law or his theology. His starting point is that the death and resurrection of Jesus are, in fact, what God has orchestrated to bring salvation, forgiveness, justification and resurrection life. This means for every one of the world's problems—think "sin" and "death"—the death and resurrection of Jesus are the solution. And God is the one who choreographed it.

This is what nerds refer to as "the Christ event." It is the fountain of the grace of God. It is the love of a God who did not spare God's own son.

Of course, whenever we're trying to make sense of something, we use the resources at our disposal. One of the most important resources for a first-century Jew like Paul was a tradition that had developed over the previous couple hundred years.

This tradition was a way of talking about martyrs. Righteous martyrs. People who were faithful to the point of death. These stories grew and flourished as Jewish people told the story of the Maccabean revolt (approximately 167–160 BCE). In that revolution, the Jewish people—who had been living under the thumb of foreign masters for hundreds of years and who had not had an army, or any military experience, for centuries—rose up and defeated a generation of warrior overlords ruled by Antiochus IV, who humbly took the moniker "Epiphanes"—god made manifest.

One famous story from that era, featured in 2 Maccabees 7, tells of seven brothers who are brought before the king to either eat pork (prohibited in Deuteronomy 14:8) or be tortured and killed.

They defy the king. As they do, they place their hope in a greater king—the King of the Universe. One by one, they express their hope that if they give their bodies for the sake of God's law, the only possible outcome is that God will honor them with restored bodies at the resurrection from the dead.

How can God be just? How can people be rewarded if they are faithful all the way to the point of death? God can raise them up. For Jews from this period, resurrection was inseparable from vindication. Resurrection meant that God had rewarded someone with a new body because that person had been faithful to the point of death. In the language of Romans, resurrection is justification.

There is another thread that runs through the martyrs' speeches. As they die for the law, they also confess that the people have not been entirely faithful to God. They interpret the rule of the tyrant Antiochus as God's judgment. God is punishing Israel through the wicked king. But they expect a reversal, a return of God's affection for the people as the people return to the law.

And their expectation is met. It's not met through the people returning *en masse* to faithfulness. It's met through the death of these righteous martyrs. Their death changes God's disposition toward the whole nation. And so we read in the chapter immediately following the martyrs' deaths, "The wrath of the Lord had turned to mercy" (2 Maccabees 8:5). In the righteous martyr tradition, the death of the faithful servant of God is both the revelation of God's wrath and the end of it.

The same story is told in 4 Maccabees. There the language comes even closer to Paul's. By enduring to "the point of death" (the same Greek phrase Paul uses to speak of Jesus in Philippians 2:8), they "vindicated" (*exedikesan*, the same Greek root as *dikaioo* that Paul uses to talk about "justification") an entire generation (4 Maccabees 17:10). How did this work? The blood of the martyrs became, through their deaths, an atoning sacrifice (*hilasterion*, the same word Paul uses to describe Jesus's death in Romans 3:25). And notice that the end result was a shift in power: no longer was their tyrannical oppressor their overlord. Sounds a lot like Romans 6–8.

Like these earlier stories, Paul never claims that God *requires* a human sacrifice in order to reconcile with humanity. Instead, he takes the fact of Jesus's resurrection to mean that something monumental happened in Jesus's death. He tells the story as one of an atoning death because he believes this is what has, in fact, happened.

Did it have to occur? I don't know. Is this what happened? Yes, according to Paul.

Sin brings guilt. Sin has power. Sin divides humanity from God and divides Jewish humanity under the law from Gentile humanity under sin. But all this is dealt with through Jesus's death on the cross and the resurrection that follows. According to Paul, God has allowed Jesus to bear our condemnation in solidarity with us (Romans 8:3) so that we can bear justification in solidarity with him.

In other words, Paul is not a good PEACH. While the death of Jesus is much bigger for him than the mere penalty-substitution we all learned about growing up, it's in no way less: Jesus bearing our guilt on the cross is as critical to Paul as Jesus freeing us from sin's enslaving power.

Bad Theology?

There's a more basic problem that has been on the front burner for many theologians for at least the past half century. When you start to break it down, the crucifixion sounds a whole lot like cosmic child abuse.

A father hands his kid over to be tortured and slaughtered so that the father can be in right relationship with other people that he is mad at. I have a friend who used to shake his head at the "bad theology" that someone deployed by saying, "You suck so God killed his kid!" Unfortunately, that "bad theology" is accurate Pauline theology.

It's "bad theology" in the sense that it is not trinitarian theology. Indeed, if there is one reason to be a trinitarian in terms of theological implications, it is that it transforms the idea of Jesus's death from God handing over another person into God handing over Godself.

Theologically, this frames the cross in a way that steps back from the otherwise all-too-apt child abuse analogy. It turns the cross into an act of self-sacrifice rather than one of other-sacrifice. It makes the cross a symbol and a story that people can be called to reenact, in order to be like God in a way that brings life to the world. It takes away the fear that someone might become like a God who makes peace by slaughtering innocents.

Unfortunately, this is not how Paul speaks of the death of Jesus. For Paul, the analogy is not "chopping off my arm," giving a part of myself, for another. For him, the story of Christ is the fulfillment of the story of Abraham. Abraham offered Isaac, and God "did not spare" Jesus. God did not "come down," God "sent his son." God did not "take on sin in human flesh," God condemned sin in the human sinful-like flesh of Jesus.

This is how Paul's story differs from the martyr tradition: God sends this martyr. It is the Messiah.

The New Testament—including the Gospels, where Jesus forgives sins during his ministry on earth—consistently depicts Jesus's death as a divine necessity. A wide array of different theological ideas arise to explain this. We have already seen two tightly intertwined in Paul's writing: Jesus died for us, to free us from condemnation; and Jesus died to the power of sin, to free us from the lordship of sin and death.

Throughout the ages, Christians have interpreted Jesus's death—its reasons, its significance and its implications for our lives—in different ways. We use the tools we have. For Paul, there were the stories of Abraham and Isaac, the Davidic psalms of deliverance from death, and the righteous martyr tradition.

For us, there is a richly developed trinitarian tradition, a more thoroughgoing recognition of the potentially lethal dynamics of familial power, and the conviction that our proclamation of God needs to mesh with what God has otherwise shown us to be true of Godself: one who desires justice, one who loves mercy. One who gave us the primal commandment not to kill. One who wants the people of the earth to embody love for one another.

Being Biblical

There are two ways to honor scripture in the attempt to live lives and articulate theologies that we might call "biblical." One way is to read the Bible, receive its conclusions and attempt to follow its commands. This is perhaps the most straightforward and safest-feeling route.

The other way is to not only receive its end points, but also to faithfully follow its process. It is to honor the active, creative work of wrestling with the implications of Jesus's life, death and resurrection that we witness in the apostles' New Testament writings and deliberations as the holy engagement to which we are called. We imitate their work rather than simply adopting their conclusions as the final, holy endpoints. The church as a whole has engaged in this second process numerous times, including when it hammered out the theology of the Trinity. This teaching is not found in scripture. However, for post-Nicene Christians who accept the story of Jesus—and the church's interpretation of it—as the saving story of God, belief in the full and singular divinity of Father, Son and Spirit has become a shared theological conclusion. This, in turn, changes what Paul's letters mean when they speak of God giving the Son. Now they can mean that the Father who is God gives the Son who is also God.

The example above is just that: an example. It shows that sometimes the contents of the Bible itself push us to say something that the Bible doesn't. And that's okay. More than okay; that's what it means to be faithfully continuing this Jesus story, which did not end in the first century. This is, really, the only way we can be "biblical."

So it's okay to acknowledge, if this is how we see it, that Paul's theology can look like divine child abuse—and that we might need to reimagine the relationship between Jesus and God so as to make clear that this is not our story.

At the same time, the cross is there. It's there as something that is ubiquitously talked about as necessary. It's violent and it's horrible. And, somehow, it's at the center of the saving story.

Perhaps we need to be careful about dismissing all of the old theology too quickly. Maybe we need the constant reminder that humanity too often and too easily goes sideways. Too readily, we rise up against our neighbors with a deep sense of self-righteousness.

Too often, we think it's only the other who needs forgiveness. And then, irony of ironies, we may find ourselves rereading Romans. Only now, we are the presumed insiders, even as the Jews were in the first century. And we may just find ourselves—those bearing the Christian name!—named as the outsiders, who by and large have rejected Jesus.

We might hear Paul whispering in our ear that another people have been brought in, while we have been left to the side. Looking for salvation in all the wrong places. Assuming we've already been saved and missing the grace of God made known in Christ.

CHAPTER ELEVEN

Romans 9: Mystery & Yearning

On Not Being a Jerk

Ah. Romans 9. How I used to love this stuff.

Back in the day, when I was first spreading my theological wings, the question of predestination was one of my favorites. I used to love getting into debates with people. "The Bible says we have free will," one really sweet man told me once. "Where does it say that?" I replied. Implied answer: nowhere.

In the debrief afterward, I would laugh with my friends that the Bible never says we have free will, but it does say we're predestined, and God chooses and it's about God's decision to make us for glory or destruction. So there.

It's hard not to become like the gods we serve. And when the God we serve is the kind of capricious jerk that I described, well, it didn't faze me when people were, shall we say, troubled by my theology. Those of us who agreed were "the believers" after all. Calvinism: winning friends and influencing people in Christian love since 1536.

So what does the much older and wiser me have to say to the young buck who loved his predestinarian theology? Two nearly opposite things that are nonetheless both true.

First, if that's what you see in Romans 9, you need to learn how to read. It is a colossal exercise in missing the point. Second, you're not all wrong. I think my younger self might have been perplexed at this point. Let me see if I can clear up what I mean.

Paul's Heartache

First, and most importantly, the self-flagellation.

In Romans 9–11, Paul is expressing and working through his heartbreak over the Jewish people, *his* people. He is wondering how it can be possible that Israel, God's chosen people, have been given the promises in scripture and covenant, and yet they are sitting on the sidelines while the Gentiles flock to Jesus as the Messiah.

"I have great sorrow and unceasing grief in my heart. I wish I could be cut off from Christ for the sake of my siblings, my kinsfolk according to the flesh" (Romans 9:2–3). Everything has been heading here: the assertion that God is just, the claim that Jesus fulfills scripture, the redefinition of "Jew" to include Gentiles who received the Spirit, the argument that Jesus's death is the mechanism for making people righteous, the re-imagining of Abraham's fatherhood as resting on God's resurrection power, and the recounting of a cosmic story of sin's guilt and power that the law could not resolve.

It's all been heading to this point where Paul grapples with the harsh reality that God's chosen people have not chosen Jesus in return. What could this mean for the Jewish people? And where could such a story be heading? Romans 9–11 was written to answer this complex question. It was *not* written to answer an academic question, nor to provide theoretical material for ponderous theology books and their reflections on the eternal, unchanging nature of God and the divine decree.

Romans 9 is the heart-rending cry for loved ones left behind. It attempts to plumb the inexplicable mystery of God showing Godself to be finally, climactically faithful to Israel while Israel itself sits to the side and waits for God to act as God has promised.

No form of Calvinism that I have met has been able to do justice to this impossible situation with its devastating grief. We pluck and pull at the threads of Romans 9 to talk about God's choice, God's glory, and human destiny. In so doing, we destroy the picture that they weave. This is a discussion of a people, first and foremost—the people of Israel.

More importantly, it is a quest for a reversal of Israel's fate; not a simple articulation of a hellacious destiny to which they have been consigned. In the end, Paul will not accept "not chosen" as the final word spoken by God over those who appear to be rejected.

There is simply too much for God to lose for the story to end with Israel's rejection. By extension, there is too much for God to lose for the story to end with the rejection of the majority of image-bearing humanity, as well.

Paul enumerates what Israel has going for it. It's a litany of divine blessings: adoption as God's children, glory, covenants, the law, promises, the ancestors and even Christ's human lineage (Romans 9:4–5).

This list is shocking. Adoption as God's children and glory are blessings that bookend the earthly life of those who are predestined by God (Romans 8:28–30). In chapter 8 they belong to those who are in Christ. But here, they are Israel's. Could they possibly be taken away? If God is for us, who can be against us?

Paul is crushed, bewildered and maybe even a little unsure. This should have been a clue to my Calvinist self that I hadn't quite taken in what Paul is serving up.

God's Choices

Secondly, alas, the Calvinists aren't completely wrong.

Paul lays out a series of illustrations to show how God chooses. (Nerds refer to this as "election.") As he does so, he picks up the arguments he made in Romans 2, that not all Israelites are Israel and not all of Abraham's descendants are the chosen children (Romans 9:7). In other words, the fact that not all individual Israelites are currently being saved is just a reflection of how God has always worked.

Paul reminds his readers that Isaac was chosen, not Ishmael (9:7–9), and Jacob was chosen over Esau (9:10–13). All were children of Abraham, but not all were the chosen line of promise. Paul provides what he understands to be the basis of this choice: it's not because of anything they had done (or had been foreseen as doing), but just so God could be the one to choose (9:11–12).

Where's the justice in that (9:14)? For Paul, it lies here: God's choosing is an act of mercy (9:15–16). Salvation, election, adoption, glory—none of these have ever come by doing the right things. They come when God chooses to rescue people who seem ill-equipped to do much of anything good. "All have sinned" (Romans 3:23). "The good that I wish I do not do, but I practice the very evil that I hate." (Romans 7:15)

In this way, too, the Law and the Prophets bear witness to the Christ to come. He brings a salvation that is not by works of the law. He is the faithfulness of Israel, offered first to Israel and then to the world as the faithfulness of God. The faithfulness of Jesus by which we are saved happens in Israel. As Messiah, like with Israel's kings of the past, what Jesus does is not only for Israel but, in a sense, as the singular embodiment of the people. His faithfulness is for his own people first and foremost ("for the Jew first," Romans 1:16). This is God's faithfulness (Romans 3:3). And it is also for the world ("and also for the Greek," Romans 1:16).

The pattern of God's choosing not only goes on after Jacob and Esau, but it intensifies. As Paul continues to skim through the early scripture stories, he comes to the Exodus. There, not only is God's son, Israel, chosen, but Pharaoh is hardened (9:17–18). Two sides of the same coin.

The same coin is where Paul's story and the Calvinists' double-predestination diverge. The later would-be interpreters of Paul see simply *divine fiat*, assigning people to one fate or another. Paul, however, sees two results that essentially depend upon each other.

For Isaac to be the heir of the promise, Ishmael cannot be. For Jacob to carry the line, Esau must be overcome. For Israel to be set free, Pharaoh must be hardened. For the cosmos to be saved, God must not spare God's own son. And, as we'll soon see, for the Gentiles to be saved, God's son, Israel, must be given up. God is not merely choosing and rejecting. God is working out salvation for God's people.

But Paul does not blunt the starkness of divine choice here in chapter 9. Instead, he amplifies it.

In verses 19–23, he introduces the image of a potter. Cue the 1990s worship band playing "Abba Father." In case you missed that one, it celebrates God as Father, who is also potter, who shapes us, the clay. The song praises God who renews us in the image of Jesus. In Romans 9, Paul celebrates God "making us beforehand for glory."

It's a beautiful sentiment, just as long as you're being molded into a Jesus-pot. But what if you're being molded into what was once affectionately termed a "piss pot" or into a spittoon? What if you're the practice run that gets tossed aside enroute to the vessel that will bring the potter glory?

Both scenarios are possible if you're a piece of clay carved off the lump and thrown on the wheel (Romans 9:20–23). God's the potter, Paul says, and God gets to choose. It's as though the bleak is somehow required for the light of glory to shine forth (9:23).

Earlier in Romans, when Paul spoke about the Law and Prophets bearing witness to the gospel story, he seems to have thought their testimony included this dark moment in Israel's own narrative. Up through verse 18, he draws on the Law (the Torah—or Pentateuch—comprising the first five books of the Bible).

When he enters a new phase of argument in verse 19, he turns to the Prophets. Paul's potter and clay material is a riff off of Isaiah 29:16. He then continues quoting and engaging the prophets with Hosea in

9:25–26 and Isaiah in 9:29–33. What, specifically, was the message of these divine heralds? First, that Israel would be culled, and only some saved. Second, that God's people will include Gentiles (9:24). There it is: the double-sided coin. The incorporation of the Gentiles is inseparable from Israel's rejection of Jesus as Messiah, and both are part of the climactic scene of salvation in the story of God and Israel.

Hosea had prophesied that God would reach out to the unloved, to those who were not God's people, and name them "Beloved" and call them "My people" (Hosea 2:25, quoted in Romans 9:25–26). Interestingly, in his recitation of Hosea's prophecy, Paul takes the words that the prophet used to describe the people Israel—who had been temporarily rejected by God and sent into exile—and applies them to the Gentiles. The Gentiles were unloved; now they are loved. The Gentiles were not God's people; now they are God's people.

Paul then quotes Isaiah 10:20–21, a text that draws on God's promise to Abraham that Israel will number the sands of the sea and ends up saying that the promise of salvation is for far fewer than that—a remnant only (Romans 9:27–28).

Two sides of one coin. The ingathering of the Gentiles, participating in Israel's blessing, while Israel itself is whittled away. If there is rejection, it is for the sake of salvation. And if there is salvation, it is for the sake of a people—a group to whom God is committed—not a smattering of individuals.

Be that as it may, what Paul says is stark. It's terrifying. Well, almost terrifying.

Back to Jesus

In the end, Paul brings it down to Jesus. Again. The refrain we've heard throughout Romans repeats itself here: The faithfulness of God is ultimately found in the faithfulness of Christ.

The Gentiles are swept up into a saving story that they were not even looking for. They are incorporated into God's righteousness.

They are justified by God's faith, made known in Christ's faith, leading them to faith (Romans 9:30). Meanwhile, Israel is stuck on a different hero. Not Christ the Messiah, by faith, but the law, by works (9:31).

In the end, Paul must return to earth from his discussions of God's heavenly purposes. And here on earth God has provided salvation for Israel. Paradoxically, this "salvation stone" is also a "stumbling stone" (9:32–33). The gift that is the fulfillment of scripture's promise of salvation is, at the same time, the offense that fulfills scripture's anticipation of rejection.

In the end, this chapter is not about the hoary, hidden decisions God makes about who gets to be part of the divine family and who gets rejected. It is about the difficulty of seeing the divine hand in the crucified Christ. It is about the obscurity of what unfolded on earth. It is about the revelation of God's good news being hidden in the proclamation of Jesus's resurrection.

"Whoever believes in him"—the stumbling stone, that is Jesus, the Messiah—"will never be put to shame" (Romans 9:33). Another scriptural quotation, this time from Isaiah 28:16.

In Isaiah, this is God's response to Israel making a "covenant with death" (Isaiah 28:15). Paul brings the text into his current situation, as we have seen him do so often before. Isaiah 28:16 becomes a statement of God's action to save in direct contravention of Israel's attempt at self-immolation. Israel's attempted failure cannot be the last word. God must provide a way out. God must be faithful.

But Israel must be willing to change its ultimate covenant allegiance. Not to a covenant with death, nor to a covenant through the law. (The two are closely joined in Romans 6–7, remember.) Instead, to the law pointing forward, bearing witness. To what? To faith: God's faith and Christ's faith. Israel must see the need for Gentiles, on this side of the Christ-event, to continue swimming in that same stream of faith.

Paul's return to earth almost undoes my original Calvinist reading of this text. Grounded in his angst for his fellow Jews and returning in the end to the Christ event as the pivotal moment on which the story turns, Paul himself is not willing to give eternal, unknown divine purpose the last word.

He returns not to what God has kept hidden, but to what God has revealed in the greatest paradox of all. (Even greater, if possible, than Israel's current state of rejecting salvation.) It is the paradox of a crucified Messiah as God's great act of salvation—the fulfillment of what God had long promised.

CHAPTER TWELVE

Romans 10: Rejecting the Gift

What Does Jesus Look Like?

Alexandria, Egypt. Early fourth century. You head down to the docks. The sailors are loading and unloading their boats. Mending sails. Braiding frayed rope.

And singing. But maybe the songs aren't what you'd expect. Think they'll be bawling out the "not-safe-for-work" fare that you'd be embarrassed if your boss or your mom overheard? Well, that all depends on who your boss and mom are, I guess, because these guys are singing Jesus songs. The bishop of Alexandria has been teaching his people well.

Hmmm. It turns out these songs are *not* safe for work, not in the fourth century, anyway. The problem is with their description of Jesus. According to the lyrics, Jesus lived with God in heaven before coming to earth—but he was not eternally preexistent with God. A council is called. "Arianism" is condemned, joyfully singing sailors be damned. Literally damned if they won't change their theology.

Are these Jesus-loving, hymn-singing sailors worthy of the condemnation they received from the church?

Durham, North Carolina. Late twentieth century. You head down to the rapidly growing church across the street. People are streaming in every Sunday. Police and volunteers are directing traffic into and out of the parking lots.

You run into an elder. Cool guy driving a cool car toting cool electronic toys. Super friendly. Welcomes you. Remembers your name. Serves the church well.

Turns out he's a surgeon at one of the local university medical centers. Also turns out that he's got a reputation for being the stereotypical god of the operating room. Intense; okay, fine. Demanding; well, he should be. But also, a complete jerk. Is this nice-on-Sundays, jerky god-of-the-operating-room worthy of the church's admiration?

How do you know faithfulness to God when you see it? Does it consist of thinking (believing) the right things? Is it shown by doing the right things? Which things would have to be believed? Which would have to be done?

For a quick snapshot of how difficult it can be to answer these questions, just remember that there are hundreds of different Christian denominations in the United States alone, and tens of thousands of other churches that are not affiliated with any of these denominations. That's hundreds of groups of churches that think they're right enough about what matters most that they need to strike out on their own rather than being affiliated with another group of churches. That's in addition to tens of thousands of churches that don't try to affiliate with anyone else at all. This is an incredible number of denominations and congregations that believe their particular points of theology are too specific, too pure for them to affiliate with anyone else.

This is just one way to show how hard it is to get consensus around the idea of what "faithful Christianity" looks like. Many of us have definite, at-the-ready responses to this question, but clearly, there is no consensus. Getting a collective grasp on it is a very difficult business.

You're Doing It Wrong

In an iconic film scene that has been life-changing for many of us, the eponymous Mr. Mom takes his kids to school for the first time. As he pulls up to the school and drives past the other cars, his kids keep telling him, "Dad, you're doing it wrong!"

Being a good, competent, insightful father, he explains, "We're going to do it the Jack Butler method!" Other cars are honking. The kids are mortified.

As he pulls up to drop off the kids, a woman in a yellow rain slicker has him roll down the window. "Hi, Jack? I'm Annette. You're doing it wrong."

Romans 10 is Paul's Annette moment. "Hi, Israel? I'm Paul. You're doing it wrong."

This is where he lays out exactly where Israel stumbled. How is it that they missed Jesus? It's not that they were too proud of being able to do what no one could. It's not that their eyes were blinded by some demonic force. It's not that God judged them as wanting and moved on to another people.

Paul says something even more difficult to hear than any of that. What did Israel do wrong? They were trying to do what the Bible told them God wanted them to do. Get your head around that if you can. Here we go.

Chapter 10 expresses Paul's heartfelt longing for Israel to come to faith in Jesus. His desire is "for salvation" (Greek *eis sōtērian*, Romans 10:1). This is the same Greek phrase he uses in Romans 1:16, when he describes the power of the gospel.

So what's the problem?

The first thing Paul says about Israel is they "[have] a zeal for God" (10:2)—just like he used to have. It was this zeal, he tells the Philippians, that led him to persecute the church (Philippians 3:6).

Maybe we're learning something here about what's driving Paul to such depths of anguish. He's not *just* lamenting the current state of his fellow Jews. He's also haunted by his own past. They are now where he once was.

Sometimes, the person we're hardest on is ourselves. What Paul learned for himself, and what he's applying to his fellow Jews, is that eagerness in the service of the one true God is not enough. God gauges faithfulness differently.

Law Pointing Beyond Itself

So what are the different matrices that Paul and his Jewish contemporaries are using to measure right standing, right action, before God? The Jews are looking to the law to show them how to act, so as to establish their righteousness as a people and as persons (Romans 10:3). In contrast, Paul insists that God's righteousness through Christ is what ultimately saves us (10:4).

Christ is the "end" of the law for righteousness to everyone who believes (Romans 3:4). Here, when Paul says "end," he probably means "goal." As we saw before in chapters 3 and 4, Paul conceives of the law as pointing beyond itself to the coming Christ. Rather than being self-referential, a list of rules to be heeded, it draws the person forward in time to a future act of God.

Paul is about to show us exactly how this works. Brace yourself.

And remember this, as we jump in: Paul's baseline conviction is that Jesus, who was crucified, is the risen Messiah. Jesus is God's way of reconciling and saving God's people. Paul interprets everything in the light of his own story, the current situation of the Jews, his hope for the Gentiles and scripture.

To draw the contrast between Jewish practice and his gospel message, Paul starts with the law. Moses, Paul asserts, states that righteousness based on the law works like this: that people who follow the dictates of the law will live by them (Romans 10:5, quoting Leviticus 18:5).

There it is. Human doing of the law.

But there's another voice to be found in scripture: the voice of "righteousness from faith." Remember what we learned in chapter one? Righteousness "from faith" means righteousness coming from *God's* faith through the faith of *Jesus*. Keep that in mind as we follow Paul's argument in Romans 10:6–13.

In these verses, he gives a step-by-step interpretation of scriptures taken from a couple of different places. He provides a running commentary on these scriptures in light of his Jesus story. This is the voice of "the righteousness from faith."

He begins by revisiting Deuteronomy 30:12: Don't say in your heart, 'Who will ascend into heaven?' Paul runs this verse through his "righteousness based on faith" filter and interprets it as warning against the attempt "to bring the Messiah (who is resurrected Lord) to earth" (Romans 10:6).

Are you sitting down?

Deuteronomy 30:12 refers to the commandments, the law given by God. When Deuteronomy says, "Don't say who will ascend into heaven" the reason it imagines for someone "going up" is to grab hold of the law and bring it down to earth: "get it for us" (Deuteronomy 30:12, NRSV). And the reason to "get it" is so that the people can hear it and do it (Deuteronomy 30:12). No one has to go up to heaven because the commandments have already been brought down by Moses. If you wanted to find a verse that said as clear as day that the whole point of the law is to receive it as given and do what it says, you could not find a better example. But Paul turns the law into a foreshadowing of Christ. Therefore, Paul argues, when Deuteronomy talks about bringing the law down, it is really bearing witness to the Christ who has already come and who will come again.

He goes on citing and interpreting: Do not say in your heart, "who will descend into the abyss?" (Deuteronomy 30:13). Which he interprets as, "To raise Christ from the dead" (Romans 10:7). This time not only does Paul insert a strange, Jesus-story reinterpretation, he even changes the wording of the verse itself. In Deuteronomy 30:13, Moses was talking about crossing the sea, not descending into its depths.

Like in the previous verse, the original context for verse 13 was that it was unnecessary for the Israelites to go fetch the law. God had already brought the law near, which made it easy to keep. (Yes, the point of Deuteronomy 30 was literally how easy God made it to keep the law. And no, this is decidedly *not* the point Paul is making when he quotes Deuteronomy 30:12–14 in Romans 10!)

By changing the language about the sea's breadth to language about its depth, Paul depicts Deuteronomy prefiguring the most important component of his gospel—God raising Jesus from the dead. Remember when I said that Jewish interpreters boldly reinterpreted the Bible based on what they believed God had done in the present? This is what I was talking about.

Paul delivers the coup de grace in Romans 10:8. He quotes Deuteronomy 30:14—"The word is near you, in your mouth and in your heart"—and equates that "word" to the faith that he is preaching (Romans 10:8). According to Paul, what do mouths and hearts have to do? The mouth needs to confess Jesus's Lordship and the heart needs to believe his resurrection (10:9). Jesus is Lord: he doesn't need to be brought down to reign, so don't ascend to heaven (10:6); God raised him from the dead, so don't descend into the abyss (10:7). This is what heart and mouth need to confess (10:8–9).

Why is this the coup de grace? Because in Deuteronomy 30:14, Moses said that the word, which is the commandment, is in your mouth and heart (the parts Paul quotes) and "in your hand, so you can do it." Paul transforms a passage about how easy it is to keep the law into a witness to the Christ who is the resurrected Lord. Then he uses this reinterpretation to show how righteousness based on faith is different from righteousness based on law. Christ is the "end" of the law (Romans 10:4). Christ is its goal. The law points to him.

Scripture after Jesus (and Paul!)

What can we learn from this? What is Israel doing wrong? They're reading and obeying scripture as if Jesus isn't the Messiah.

Paul continues drawing on scripture to prove that righteousness and salvation come from faith, trust and confession that Jesus is Lord. He cites Isaiah 28:16, as he did at the end of chapter 9, when he claims that no one who believes and trusts in God will be put to shame at the final judgment (Romans 10:11).

Why does Paul use the language of "shame" here? In many "western" cultures we have a deep tradition of guilt for wrongdoing that is often read into the more interpersonal language of shame. Part of what is entailed in honor versus shame in the first century Mediterranean world is a person fulfilling their obligations to those over them and under them in society. In this case, people who trust in God have hope that they will not be shamed before God at the final judgment. This means they will be proven to have acted in accordance with their obligations toward God, and God will also fulfill God's obligations toward them in extending final salvation.

Faithfulness to the Jesus story is how Paul understands the obligation that humanity bears in its relationship to God. This is where the confidence comes from that they will not be ashamed.

He then goes on to cite Joel 2:32 to demonstrate that Jews and Gentiles have equal access to God: whoever calls on the name of the Lord will be saved (Romans 10:13). "The name of the Lord"—that's the heart of the matter. For Paul, the name of the Lord is "Jesus." This is where Israel is not on board.

These verses provide a transition into a new line of Paul's argument. Scripture foreshadows not only Jesus, but the very situation Paul finds himself in: Jews rejecting the gospel while Gentiles stream in.

What's the current context? The gospel has gone out into all the world, as proclaimed in Psalm 19:4 (Romans 10:18). Israel has heard. So why didn't they come around? That's part of scriptural prophecy, as well. In Deuteronomy 32:21, Moses foretold that God would make Israel jealous by redirecting divine affections toward another people (Romans 10:19).

Remember this one! It is going to be critical to understanding Romans 11. Paul believes that the massive influx of Gentiles will make the Jews jealous, prompting them to follow the Gentiles into the fold.

Isaiah also anticipates people who weren't seeking after God would find God (Isaiah 65:1, quoted in Romans 10:20). That would be the Gentiles. Note that this is the opposite of where we started in chapter 10: Israel was seeking zealously after God but did not find God's way of righteousness. Now, those who were not seeking have found God, through God's Messiah.

Isaiah goes on in the next verse to lament that Israel rejects the divine overtures (Isaiah 65:2, quoted in Romans 10:21). This is exactly the situation Paul believes he finds himself in.

From Scripture to Life: Jesus, Again

In the end, how are we supposed to know what faithfulness to God looks like? For Paul, it looks like recognizing the crucified Christ as the resurrected Lord. It looks like responding to this message of God's surprising manifestation of righteousness.

It's not simply about having faith [full stop] versus working for salvation [full stop]. It's an invitation to see the faith of God in the faith of Christ and to entrust ourselves to this story of salvation. Paul isn't trying to persuade his readers to change which part of themselves they use in their hopes of pleasing God (thinking/believing the right things rather than doing the right things). He is trying to get Israel to entrust themselves to the work that is done in and through Christ, rather than in and through the law.

Why is this the right thing? And how does Paul know?

Because Christ was not put to shame before God. Because Christ was saved from death. Because Christ was declared righteous.

In other words, because of the resurrection. That changed everything for Paul. Which is why he needs it to change everything for his fellow Jews, as well.

CHAPTER THIRTEEN

Romans 11: What Hope Remains for Israel?

Endings

Like many a high school and college student, I once had an unhealthy obsession with *Monty Python and the Holy Grail*. Migrating coconuts. Supreme executive power deriving from a mandate from the masses, not some farcical aquatic ceremony. Shrubbery. The whole nine yards.[1]

I developed this obsession, as everyone must, despite the brutal betrayal that is foisted upon the audience in the final scene. Without giving too much away, it's not too much to say that the film doesn't end; it just stops.

The story doesn't resolve. Anything you might have anticipated coming to pass is left lingering. It leaves you with the hollow emptiness of unfulfilled hope.

The specter of just such an ending—for Israel—seems to be driving Paul throughout Romans. He must, and does, believe that God, as the author of Israel's script, will not allow their role in the story to

---

[1] You're welcome for not saying, "The full monty."

simply ... stop. Israel cannot be cast out of the storyline like a dead character whose actor didn't get her contract renewed. It must have a future.

That's what Paul explores in Romans 11. What are the implications if Israel's current experience is just the latest installment in a history of those not chosen? How can this be, if they are in the line of promise (Romans 9)? What does it mean that Israel is fulfilling the scriptural precedent of turning away from God at the very moment when God is extending saving hands to the world (Romans 10)? How can there be a future in Christ for a people who have rejected Jesus as the Messiah?

Paul anticipates an ending to the story. It's an ending that is much more this-worldly than many interpreters of Romans 11 have found. He does not expect salvation for each and every Jew. He does not expect a mass conversion at the moment when Jesus returns from heaven.

Instead, he expects that the plan of God now entails Gentiles preceding Jews, and that the Gentile mission itself will be a catalyst spurring Israel to faith. It's supposed to get into Israel's craw and lead them to repentance. "I will make you jealous by those who are not a nation" (Deuteronomy 32:21; Romans 10:19).

All Are Not Lost

Paul claims that Israel as a whole is not rejected. In fact, there is a faithful remnant. This, he argues, is in keeping with scripture—it happened before in the days of Elijah; it is happening now, as he himself is part of the faithful (Romans 11:1–5).

He then rehearses the idea that only some are saved because salvation is by grace, not by works (11:6). Being faithfully Jewish is not enough to enter into the promises of the Jewish God.

But more than this, Paul attributes the ingathering of some and the falling away of others as an act of divine election. He cites scripture that speaks of God giving the people of Israel eyes and ears that do not perceive (Romans 11:8, citing Deuteronomy 29:4). Like Romans 9, this is a story of God keeping people away on purpose. And like Romans 10, Romans 11 chronicles how the scriptures are being fulfilled among the Jewish people, during the time of Paul.

Paul then cites retributive verses from a psalm of David (Romans 11:9–10, citing Psalm 69:22–23). David prayed for the enemies of God's people to have darkened eyes and bent backs. Stark words.

In a sense, these early verses of chapter 11 are rehearsing what Paul has said before, and lending more scriptural weight to his rendering of Israel's story. He is not yet offering a solution. If anything, he continues to underscore the problem and God's role in it, bending the story until it seems it must break and relieving the tension with only the slightest glimmers of hope. Then, he begins to build his argument about Israel's future.

Remember how Paul had cited Isaiah in chapter 9: "They stumbled over the stumbling stone." Now, he rhetorically asks, "They didn't stumble all the way to falling, did they?" (Romans 11:11).

And that's where hope begins.

No, says Paul. They didn't.

So what's going on? Salvation has come to the Gentiles to make Israel jealous (11:11). See? I told you we would see that jealousy argument again.

Rejection with a Purpose

But then Paul shifts the focus back to the Gentiles. He shows that Israel's rejection of Jesus as messiah has led to a wealth of blessings for the nations and he anticipates that even more blessings will come when the full number of Jews joins the community of faith (11:12). (This is typical ancient Jewish rhetoric: argue from the lesser thing to the greater thing. If this apparently worthless event of Israel's disinterest leads to Gentile riches, how much more will the Gentiles be enriched by the amazing act of Israel's convergence around the resurrected Jesus.)

Don't think this is happening without Paul in the middle of it! He's talking to Gentiles (11:13) and exalting his ministry in the hopes of moving his own flesh, the Jewish people, to jealousy—and from jealousy to salvation (11:14).

Jealousy. There it is again. The Jews will be jealous, and not just because some Gentiles out there, in some far away time and place, will worship Israel's God. They will be jealous because of what Paul has managed to accomplish among the Gentiles. Paul is the one whose work leads to Gentile inclusion. The fruit of Paul's work is *supposed* to move Israel to jealousy. Paul believes God is using him to create the conditions needed to bring Israel to repentance. He hopes that Israel will want a piece of what the Gentiles have taken hold of.

Israel Embodying the Jesus Story

Perhaps Paul's most profound theological reflection on Israel's current state of hardening and partial rejection by God is found in his brief words in verse 11:15: If their rejection is the reconciliation of the cosmos, what will their acceptance be if not life from the dead?

Israel's own story, including its darkness and rejection, is an embodiment of the Jesus story. Jesus himself was rejected, abandoned on the cross. "My God, my God, why have you forsaken me?" His was an act of self-giving obedience—and also an act of God, who handed over the beloved son. This act brought both righteousness and reconciliation.

Now here is Israel, in their estrangement from God. And the result? The reconciliation of the cosmos, through the gospel message. Israel as forsaken son of God is continuing the work that Jesus began as forsaken son of God. But the story of Jesus did not end on the cross.

The only reason Paul thinks anything good came from the cross is that Jesus was raised from the dead. Jesus was appointed son of God with power. He embodied—quite literally—a new humanity, one God wants all to conform to.

So now we see the shape of Paul's hope for Israel. For Israel, to whom "belong adoption as sons" (Rom 9:4), they who are the "firstborn son" of God (Exodus 4:22–23). Yes, the rejection of God's firstborn son is the reconciliation of the world. But God has not abandoned Israel.

So what will their acceptance look like? Life from death (Romans 11:15), even as it was for the beloved son whom God did not spare but delivered up for us all (8:32). The Jesus story helps Paul interpret not only Israel's past, in its scriptures, but its present and its hope. Theirs is a Christ-hope. Paul hopes for Israel as Abraham hoped for Isaac: hope for life from the hand of the God who gives life to the dead.

Interlopers Beware

Hoping in God is good and right and boasting in God is fine. But, warns Paul, Gentile readers shouldn't boast over Israel, as if this was their story to begin with. It's not. It's Israel's. The Gentiles are the interlopers.

Some may have fallen away: branches were broken off (11:17). And Gentiles may have slipped in: branches grafted into the spots left behind (11:17–19). But God is able to reverse both of these processes (11:20–21). The hope is not to watch Israel wither. It would be anti-Christian to delight in Jews standing outside the community of those who name Jesus as Messiah. Paul longs to see them grafted back on the stalk, which is theirs by rights (11:19–24).

Yet there is a peculiar necessity that Paul sees at work. For some mysterious reason, the Israelite branches need to be removed in order to allow in the Gentile branches. It's not only what happened, not merely ordering one before the other in time: for Paul, it is a heart-wrenching necessity.

Jesus had to be rejected for the salvation of humanity.

Israel had to be rejected for the reconciliation of the nations.

Once More, with Gusto

Paul tells the story yet again, beginning in verse 25. Israel has been hardened. The result? The full number of Gentiles now may come into

God's new humanity (11:25). And what does this in turn lead to? "All Israel will be saved" (11:26).

What does "all Israel" mean? In all likelihood, it refers to the full number of Jews who, like Paul, come to put their faith in Jesus as the answer to God's promises. Paul is just warming up this argument in the beginning of chapter 9, when he says that not all who are descended from Israel are truly Israel (9:6). Toward the end of chapter 9, he cites Isaiah's prophecy that only a remnant will be saved from Israel (9:27). Having gone through all the ways that Israel has rejected the message, Paul now articulates his hope that there will be a massive turning of the Israelites to Jesus as Messiah. "All" Israel means the large number who will enter.

What does Paul mean when he says, "in this way all Israel will be saved" (Romans 11:26)? He is still talking about the process that he's been envisioning throughout the chapter, namely that each group allows for or causes the salvation of the other. The Jews are hardened, so the Gentiles come in. The world had already seen this. It's what Paul is grappling with throughout chapters 9–11. There is one step in this prophecy that has not yet been fulfilled. All that remains is the outcome precipitated by the Gentiles coming in: that the Jews get jealous and join them. There's a mutual dependence leading to this one new people.

Paul bolsters this by citing a scripture passage that, he claims, proves that this is how salvation works: "The deliverer will go forth out of Zion, he will remove ungodliness from Jacob, and this is my covenant with them when I take away their sins" (Romans 11:26–27, citing Isaiah 59:20–21, 27:9). Remember that this verse is supposed to uphold the idea that Jews are rejected, leading to Gentile inclusion, which in turn leads to Jews being drawn in so that "all Israel" will be saved. With that in mind, the passage in Romans now sounds like this:

1. "The deliverer will go forth out of Zion." Jesus goes forth, away from Israel to the Gentiles. This happens through Paul's mission.

2. "He will remove ungodliness from Jacob." Paul reads this clause in sequence with the preceding one. After the deliverer goes

out of Zion (clause 1) he then comes back to remove ungodliness from Jacob. As Paul articulates his hope in Romans 11, this happens as Israel gets jealous of the Gentiles.

3. "This is my covenant with them when I take away their sin." God has taken away sin through the death of Jesus.

At this time in the cosmic story—the time of sin being done away—these are the steps for the salvation of the Jews and Gentiles alike: Gentiles first, then the Jews.

Notice that there's no indication that Jesus has to come to earth from some "heavenly Zion." Paul's argument is much more mundane. This whole business of Israel's restoration all happens around his own mission. In fact, Paul alters the passage from Isaiah 59 so that it fits his narrative more smoothly. According to the Greek translation (which is what Paul cites), the deliverer will come *for the sake of* (Greek: *heneken*) Zion. But that's not what Paul says. According to the Hebrew translation (which is what most of our Old Testament translations are based on), the deliverer will come *to* (Hebrew: *l-*) Zion. But that's not what Paul says, either. Paul is reading this passage in light of what has actually happened: the Messiah has departed *from* (Greek: *ek*) Zion/Jerusalem. Those are the words he uses. The Messiah has gone out from among the Jews in Galilee and Judea, leaving them aside for the time being, in order to bring in the Gentiles. So Paul hopes for Christ to return and remove ungodliness from Jacob—the chosen line of the covenant promise.

One Last Time—Just to Be Sure

As if to underscore the point that this all happens due to the spreading of God's grace here below, and not some yet-to-come descent of Jesus from heaven, Paul reiterates his argument. Yes, this is like the tenth time. Cut the guy some slack. I mean, most people still don't understand his point despite him telling us over and over, so ...

Speaking to his Gentile readers, he says, "They are enemies for your sake" (Romans 11:28). Jewish rejection made it possible for the Gentiles to be embraced. And God still loves the Jews (11:29).

Then there's that causation again: They were disobedient *so that* you could be obedient (11:30). And vice versa: you have been shown mercy *so that* they can be shown mercy (11:31).

What happens when you do away with the law as God's divine standard? Israel rejects the message, which means that everyone stands on the level ground of disobedience—and God can show mercy to all (11:32).

Mystery and Wonder in The End

After laying out all of his mini-arguments about why the Jewish people are in the situation they find themselves in, perhaps Paul feels the weight of how inadequate these explanations are. In the end, he steps back to praise.

> Oh, the depths of the riches of both the wisdom and knowledge of God!
> How unsearchable are God's judgments.
> How incomprehensible are God's ways.
> "For who has known the mind of the Lord?
> Or who became God's counselor?" (quoting Isaiah 40:13)
> "Or who has first given to God and then been paid back?" (quoting Job 41:11[2])

---

[2] Ok, it's a little more complicated. Paul is not citing from the Hebrew text, which is what most of our English translations of Job are made from. He's citing a Greek translation of Job, which has interpreted the verse differently from the Hebrew. Also, the numbering is different. So, it all boils down to this: Paul is citing Job 41:3 in the Greek which is actually Job 41:11 in the Hebrew except that it says something completely different.

Because from God, and through God, and to God are all things.
To God be the glory forever. Amen. (Romans 11:33–36)

That's how Paul brings his most important theological argument (chapters 9–11) to a close: a psalm of praise. The idea that God would reject Israel, the first-born son, for a time in order to reconcile the world is unexpected. It's mind-boggling. It's incomprehensible. It's as startling as the idea that God would reject the Messiah, God's son, for a time in order to bring about righteousness and reconciliation. The only thing more difficult to grasp is that Israel is saved by Gentile inclusion.

So Paul praises God using words from scripture that probe similar mysteries. He quotes Isaiah, who prophesied that a remnant would be saved out of Israel's vast number and said that we can only hope to learn the Lord's mind; we don't get to set the plans. This is what Paul has been trying to do throughout Romans: understand in retrospect what it is that God is up to. Paul then consults Job, the ultimate book for those wrestling with God's apparent rejection of faithful, righteous servants. In the end, Paul concludes, all things are God's to do with as God wills. Sometimes mystery is all we have.

Paul's song of praise in chapter 11, like the larger argument that brings the letter to its climax here, is inextricably entwined with the argument he's been making in chapters 1 through 8. Driving the entire letter is the question of how Jews and Gentiles, in their respective relationships with God, show us who God is and what God is up to in the world. The dream is for one, unified people. The reality is far different.

Paul is trying to hold onto as much of the original story as he possibly can. The Jewish roots of his message are palpable in nearly every line he writes, and he cites scripture over fifty separate times. But the recipients of his letter, like most who have embraced his message, are not naturally borne from that root stock. They are the grafted-in Gentiles, who must learn what it is to be both the majority and the outsiders, to celebrate what God has given them and mourn for what is missing.

Paul himself holds onto God as the one who is faithful and righteous, both by celebrating the Gentile mission and by hoping and pleading for a different future for his own people. Paul vindicates God by naming the mystery of Israel's circumstance as an embodiment of the Jesus-story: rejected and "dead" as instruments of salvation, hoping to rise again and experience the love of God in Christ. God is not finished with Israel.

Paul's next task is to articulate how a people composed of both Jews and Gentiles can live together in the world. What does faithfulness to God look like when it's embedded in a community?

Those are the questions for Romans 12–15.

CHAPTER FOURTEEN

Romans 12–13: Living the Jesus Story: From Death to Resurrection

Story Starters

People who found a thing typically get to set its culture. I can't tell you how many times I've heard pastors say to their church plant that no other congregation is like this one—it's just the best. They say it like it's a big compliment, but I always think, "Yeah, that's because you made it just the way you like it!"

My dad talked about ship captains in a similar way. He would sometimes reflect wistfully about the honor and weighty responsibility of being a ship's first commanding officer. Each ship has its own reputation—which is to say, it has its own culture. And that culture is set at the beginning. How that ship's story starts is going to be how it continues. Or, if it changes, that reworking will be the labor of years. Especially if it's to be a change for the better.

Beginnings are critical. They frame the narratives we tell ourselves. Whether it's the beginning of a relationship ("Tell me how you met your partner"), or a company ("How did you come up with that idea?"), or a movement ("When did you know you had to get out the door and into the streets?").

Romans 12–15 provides a blueprint of sorts for Paul's ideal culture for the church. In establishing this, he is guided by the foundations of the movement: those moments that create the DNA that will be perpetuated throughout the life of the community. He looks back to the self-sacrificial love of Christ. He draws from the Christ-honoring resurrection by the Spirit, and the formation of a family in which Jews and Gentiles alike are reckoned to be faithful children of God.

Paul has spent the first eleven chapters laying out significant moments of this story and their implications. Now it's time to develop the implications for our life together.

"Therefore."

That's how chapter 12 begins.

"Therefore" is an invitation to connect the dots, to learn together what it looks like to live as the Jesus people. The chapters that follow lay out what we should be seeing and doing if the Spirit truly has given us victory over sin and death (building on Romans 5–8). They depict the surprising, diverse, expansive community that we belong to as the people of God (building on Romans 9–11). They describe the life of faithfulness, morality and ethics that is created after the law no longer governs us.

If this "therefore" means anything, then the result will not be a vanilla "Judeo-Christian ethic." Paul's whole point is that the arrival of Jesus changes everything. We don't look to Moses to set our trajectory; we look to the resurrected Lord Jesus. Jesus "stands up the ship" of Christianity, giving it the culture that should endure throughout the ages. The Christ-event is the narrative that gives the church's story its shape.

Both our lives as individual persons and our life together as a people of God should tell the Jesus story. They should look particular and weird. How does Paul put it?

Therefore, present your bodies as a living sacrifice (Romans 12:1). Each of you. All of us.

The foundational commandment of our life together is to narrate the Jesus story. We are to embody Jesus's sacrifice. But we're dead while still living here on earth: the living dead.

This is worship (12:1). Full worship in the biblical tradition always included sacrifice. Today, the sacrificial victim is no longer an animal; it is our very lives. It is no longer the book of the law that instructs us in how to worship God; it is the book of the Christ event. This pleases God (12:1).

This just in from our "For What It's Worth" department: Jesus thought his followers should look like this, too. "All who would be my disciples must deny themselves, take up their crosses and follow me" (Mark 8:34). Whether you're reading Paul's letters or the Gospel stories, a life that looks like the crucified Christ is the first word on what it means to live as a faithful follower of Jesus.

Therefore, "don't be conformed to this world, but be transformed by the renewing of your mind" (Romans 12:2).

Once again, Paul sends us back, this time to Romans 7–8. The power of the Spirit causes a mental transformation—a new way of thinking and being that overcomes the sinful flesh. And we are capable of living into it. The Spirit enables us to know the good and perfect will of God (12:2).

Remember chapter 8? The chapter that was all about transformation but didn't have any imperatives? Here they are, in chapter 12. This is what transformed life looks like. We see it in the death and resurrection of Jesus. We are called to embody it by laying down our lives as an act of worship.

Jesus People in Context

Verses 3–20 can sound like pretty straightforward instructions that don't need much context: don't be full of yourself (12:3); recognize that there's different stuff for each of us to do depending on the gifts God gives (12:4–8, the lesser-known cousin of the "gifts in the body of Christ" talk that Paul gives in 1 Corinthians 12); be good to each other (12:9–20).

But let's remember where we are. Paul has just delivered a lengthy argument about how God's actions transform the identity of God's people. This "people" consists of many Gentiles and far too few Jews. Paul has warned the Gentiles against becoming arrogant and boasting over the Jews (11:18). And earlier, Paul had warned the Jews that the "law" of faith precludes them boasting in the law (3:27).

Arrogance and contempt take on a very particular cast in light of Paul's rebukes. His admonitions in chapter 12 are a deliberate warning for those groups who are tempted to believe they bear some singular mark of divine favor.

Gentiles have their reasons. Jews have theirs. Paul has attempted to level it all. Therefore, let no one think more highly of themselves than is fitting; don't be cocky (12:3, 16).

These instructions recall the work of the Spirit in forming the people of God. Paul's most characteristic way of describing salvation is in terms of "union with Christ" or being "in Christ." This is the work of the Spirit (see Romans 8:9). And it makes us Christ's body (12:4).

So *we* are Christ's body. And *I* am Christ's body. And *you* are Christ's body. It's what we are collectively and what we are individually.

Which all means that we are members *of one another*, in addition to being members of Christ. Incidentally, this is why the Jesus story must be embodied in each of us individually and in our community together. Because who we are is none other than the crucified and risen Christ.

Therefore, we are called to re-narrate his story in our own lives. This means humility (12:3). This means knowing what we are gifted to do (12:4–8). This means giving to each other as needs arise (12:8, 13). This means empathy: rejoicing with those who rejoice, weeping with those who weep (12:15).

This also means taking on the posture of Christ Crucified when facing persecution. The posture of the one who prayed from the cross, "Father, forgive them, for they know not what they do" (Luke 23:34). Living out the Jesus story means not repaying evil for evil (Romans 12:17). It means doing good to all and being at peace so far as it is up to us (12:17–18).

Peace

Pause. Let's sit with this one.

I have a very strong conviction that Christians should be known for being odd. We should be weird because Jesus is calling us to something radically countercultural. Too often, however, we're known for the *wrong* weird things.

Because the *right* weird things are so hard, so counterintuitive, that sometimes even we cannot see them ourselves.

Case in point: For those of us who live in America, and more generally, those who live in communication-age western societies, violence is a core part of our identity. It is part of what we think makes our country great. It is how we imagine enforcing peace. We often reward people who bully their way to the top—those who engage in social, emotional and vocational violence, as much as those who wield weapons.

Our identities are tied to sports teams whose violence leaves the players with aching bodies, depleted minds and early deaths. Violence and bullying are associated with manliness, power, and strength.

So where does this leave Christians?

One of our recurring failures is that we have not created communities that offer an alternative reality—the reality of the cross, the reality of a God who brings justice by giving life to the dead. In other words, instead of living as Christ-followers, we have placed a Jesus-label on the destructive patterns of the world.

We have not been transformed by the renewing of our minds.

It is not godly to destroy someone who comes for us first. It's never righteous, even if it may be justified. It is not godly to settle disputes by force of arms. There is no such thing as a just war in the kingdom of God, whatever our justifications may be here on earth.

Here's the thing about the story of the cross. The cross takes two. It takes a crucifier and a crucified. All too often those bearing the power and privilege of the crucifier perceive themselves to be the crucified. This is particularly true in the church. So let me offer you a measuring stick, something we can use to gauge whether we and our communities are living out the Jesus narrative. In any given situation, ask this: Are my circumstances reflective of the crucified Christ? Or am I playing the part of the crucifying soldier?

If we put that question to ourselves honestly—be it in our day-to-day interactions with our neighbors or business partners, in our church activities or membership requirements, in our politics or decisions on how to respond to a global pandemic—if we put that question to ourselves honestly, the narrow way of Jesus will usually become clear.

Unpause.

Paul goes on: Don't take your own revenge. Leave room for the wrath of God (12:19).

No revenge? Don't defend myself? Be at peace? Who on earth would want to be a part of that story?

Anyone who is not interested has shown their shame of the cross of Christ. Jesus says he will return this shame toward such people in the final judgment (Mark 8:38). Maybe my little digression there wasn't so much of a digression after all.

A large swath of American Christianity has established a narrative in which sexual temptation is the biggest obstacle to living faithfully in Christ. But in reality, violence and power lure far more of us off the narrow path. The way of peace is too difficult. And so, we name the culture we have inherited—the patterns of this world (12:2)—"Christianity," and count Jesus among its proponents. All the while, Jesus is someplace quite distant, walking the narrow road with the faithful few willing to live lives transformed by the cross.

What are we to do? Do not be overcome by evil but overcome evil with good (12:21).

Being Subject to Rulers

With all this talk about embodying the Jesus story, it is perhaps not surprising that Paul tells his readers to be subject to the governors and rulers (13:1–7). After all, Jesus did this. He spoke the truth but was subject to their authority. He found money to pay the temple tax (Matthew 17:27). And in the end, of course, he was submissive even to the point of death on a cross.

Fine. But then, strangely, Paul goes on to say that submitting to authorities is totally no big deal, that good things will happen if you're a law-abiding person (Romans 13:3–5). That doesn't sound like the Jesus story.

Paul's claim is founded on his conviction that God (who is, after all, the king of the cosmos) is the one who gives human rulers their authority (13:1–2). It's almost like there is an upward-flow of power and submission.

What Paul is saying isn't that hard to get our heads around. What to do with it, however, is a bit complicated.

Here's the first thing. As Paul articulates fully in 1 and 2 Corinthians (and especially in 1 Corinthians 1), the gospel story—you remember, the story in which the person who was rejected, beaten, downtrodden, shamed and killed then became Lord of all—turns the world's power structures on their heads. "Up" isn't "up" anymore. Up is down and down is up. To find Jesus—to find God!—you have to look down the pecking order to the child (Mark 9:37).

In other words, Paul's advice to submit in hopes of authorities being nice to you isn't very gospel-y. It hasn't been transformed by the power dynamics of the gospel story that Paul insists on so thoroughly elsewhere. Yes, it's good advice to set the context for people who should be expecting to suffer as Jesus did to re-narrate his crucifixion story. But it's missing the massive political upheaval signaled in the act of calling the crucified Jesus Lord.

The other thing that complicates how Romans 13 is read in democratic societies is our comparative ability to participate in government. To choose our leaders. Yes, we submit to the rule of the presidents and prime ministers we did not elect. But we also protest their actions.

We get different political leaders to help us stand against and change the laws that countermand the divine requirement to love our neighbor as ourselves.

In other words, when getting guidance from scripture on how to engage our political context, we need to start by recognizing that our situation would be completely inconceivable to Paul. We vote for our leaders. We have an assumed right to participate in the political decision-making process. My suggestion, therefore, is this: rather than taking Paul's conclusions about government as our starting point, let's use the guiding framework he has given us. Let's take hold of the Jesus story—the story of sacrificial love creating a reconciled humanity and cosmos—and figure out what the implications are.

In our politics, let's ask what it looks like to play the role of the crucified Christ, willing to lay down our lives so that others might live. In our local, national and global conversations, when we're staking out the nature of our politics and our hopes for the world, let's ask what it looks like to love our neighbors as ourselves.

In the meantime, actions such as paying taxes and obeying just laws are good for our neighbors and good for society. Bearing that "cross," even when it's uncomfortable to our own bottom line or our own preferences, may just be part of what being the Jesus-body looks like.

Neighbors

I've mentioned neighbors a couple times. That was foreshadowing. Hope you caught it. Because in verses 8–11, we learn that loving our neighbors summarizes what this life of ours is supposed to be.

We should be playing the part of the crucified Christ rather than the crucifying Roman. This should be our politics. Paul says here that the saying, "Love your neighbor as yourself" is the fulness of the law (Romans 13:8).

Yes, that's right; there's a final connection here between the law and the Christian. And it's not negative. It's not just for Jews. The law is a guide, a good thing.

How is that coherent with what Paul has said before? Remember this: the function of the law is to point ahead to Christ, to witness what is to come. We have heard that witness in the foreshadowing of the resurrection (Romans 4) and Jesus's enthronement as Lord (Romans 10).

So what if the cross itself is the consummate act of love? What if Jesus's laying down his life so that others might live is what it ultimately looks like to "love your neighbor as yourself"?

If we love like that, we will not commit adultery. If we love like that, we will not kill. If we love like that, we will not steal. If we love like that, we will not covet (Romans 13:9).

As the body of the crucified Christ, we can embody the fullness of the law. We do this by loving our neighbors as ourselves. And thus, the commandments find their embodiment in the Christ story.

From Death to Resurrection

The instructions that begin in 12:1 with an admonition to don Jesus's death conclude in 13:11–14 with an encouragement to lay hold of his resurrection and the new creation. According to the great clock of the universe, it is time to arise from sleep (13:11). This means that the day of salvation is near (13:11).

Extending this day and night imagery, Paul declares that a life wrapped up in loving our neighbors is work suitable to the daytime— the time of God's great and final visitation to make all things new. And as we learned in Romans 8, the new day dawning is the day of full and final salvation, not merely for us as persons but for the cosmos.

The "weapons of light" that Paul calls us to put on (13:12) recall the weapons of righteousness—aka our bodies—that he called on us to present to God back in Romans 6. Here, as there, to walk in the light means to take hold of our future and bring it to bear on the present. This is now a betrayal of the call to peace that we talked about earlier. Paul uses the language of weaponry as a metaphor for "combating" whatever does not resemble love for our neighbors (like war).

We are to grab hold of the resurrection life that awaits us and make it the life we live here and now. We are to be the body of the resurrected, not merely crucified, Christ. This is why Paul ends with this injunction: Put on the Lord Jesus Christ and take no care to provide for the lusts of the flesh (13:14).

The Lord Jesus Christ is the resurrected One. The One who died has been justified from sin (Romans 6:7). To live the life of neighbor love that Paul is calling us to is to enable the new day to dawn before it fully arrives. This is the weird that Christianity should be. The weird of daylight for those who have too long dwelt in the night.

CHAPTER FIFTEEN

Romans 14:1–15:13: One Body. Really.

Food Matters

It's Thanksgiving. The turkey has been cooking for a few hours. It's not my house, so I've been a bit anxious about that one. There are those who believe that their great service to humanity is cooking all animal products until said products are so far from being able to support microbial life that they are quite incapable of bringing life to one's tastebuds, either. I live in terror of this.

Pushing this fear to the back of my mind, I am otherwise beyond excited.

Yeast rolls, sweet potato casserole, brussels sprouts hash, and that random green Jell-O salad that someone's mom has been making since the 1970s—simultaneously oh so good and terrible. Oh, and please, don't forget the gravy.

But then …

Then the food is served. And the drink. And that's when the crushing reality of celebrating Thanksgiving in Alabama with my wonderful, conservative Baptist in-laws lands its blow. No wine.

How can I communicate the extent to which this rips the soul out of my meal? For me, a feast without wine is like everyone remaining seated through the "Hallelujah" chorus. I mean, if you're not going to have wine with a feast, you might as well just pour a bowl of Cheerios.

As you might suspect, I emerged from this experience a changed man. For instance, never again would we celebrate Thanksgiving with this side of the family without a secret collaboration among my wife's sister and cousins that has us all drinking undisclosed beverages out of metal water bottles.

Food matters. What we drink matters. Because the facts of calories and nutritional needs don't begin to touch on the ways that we express our identity through food. We are what we eat.

What we eat ties us to our family of origin. It marks tradition. It is part of culture that defines us in ways we sometimes don't even realize until it's not there anymore.

Food is deeply personal.

And when we have the luxury of choice, deciding *not* to eat something can have just as powerful an effect. Some people forgo certain foods for personal health reasons, or to preserve the environment. Some say no in order to honor God. Some abstain permanently, swearing off alcohol or embracing vegetarianism as a lifelong commitment. Others abstain for a time, fasting as an expression of religious devotion.

In these and countless other complicated ways, food is life. Not just for the ongoing maintenance of our bodies, but *life*. It is a part of our joy. It is a part of our discipline. Sometimes a gift and an ally. Sometimes a bane and a nemesis.

Think back to that teetotaling Thanksgiving. You might say that I was eager to live life to the fullest, and I felt that a piece of life was being taken away.

You might say that my in-laws were committed to dying to the desires of the flesh, and for them, alcohol would not have been life at all.

Paul tells us in Romans 14 that there's Jesus enough for both. And in the context of, yes, food, he tells us that life and death are indeed at stake. And that's okay. Because Jesus both died and lived again—so he could be Lord of both the dead and the living (14:9).

Food is Life—and Religion

As we get into these last couple of chapters, let's remind ourselves for the umpteenth time that the critical, on-the-ground, heart-wrenching issue driving the whole letter is the status of the Jewish people before God. What can it possibly mean to say that the Jewish messiah has come, but the Gentiles—not the Jews—are the ones who are serving him?

This is not merely a theoretical question. Because life on the ground is different when mostly non-Jewish people make up the community. The Gentiles came to the faith after serving different gods; they came with a different culture. And the differences were thoroughly religious.

In the first century, three everyday practices set apart the Jewish people as unique: circumcision, food laws and Sabbath observance (not just keeping one day in seven holy but keeping all of the Jewish special holidays). With this in mind, we can see that Romans 14:1–15:13 is a guide for Jews and Gentiles living together. Serving Jesus together, in life and in death.

Do we have to die to the yummy food, or can we live and enjoy it? The answer to this, as with most either/or questions, is yes. Do we have to rest one day in seven, or can we maintain a pattern of work and play that lets us get more time with our non-Jesus-y family? Yes.

Yes, do what you need to do, but remember that first, you must love and accept each other. You need to become the kind of community that displays to the world the narrative of the crucified and risen Christ—the one who died and lived so that he might accept all of us, Jew and Gentile alike, into the family of God (Romans 15:7).

Weak and Strong

There's a rift in this community. As we've seen, Paul is addressing Gentiles throughout the letter, and he's also wrestling with the fate of Israel. And he's been telling Gentiles how to think about themselves as newcomers in this story. Way back in my introductory comments about the situation in Rome, I pointed out that there is evidence of Jews (perhaps including the famous Priscilla and Aquila[1]) who were kicked out of Rome and then later allowed to return. It may well be that the Gentiles Paul is writing to are suddenly confronted with having to figure out how to relate to these Jews whose story they've adopted–especially those who follow Jesus.

As it turns out, there is some on-the-ground trouble. Romans is not just a theological exploration of Israel's identity and God's action. It's a letter aimed at forming, and reforming, the church in Rome. We learn in chapters 14–15 that there is a rift that falls along the lines of Jewish law observance. Paul calls the parties to this debate "the weak" and "the strong." That choice of labels doesn't sound like a recipe for mutuality. And maybe it was a tactical mistake.

I know what you're thinking, and it's my first thought, too: It's pretty condescending to call people with a different opinion "the weak ones." But let's also remember that Paul is proclaiming a crucified Messiah and boasts in weakness as part of his regular apostolic repertoire (see, for instance, every single verse of 2 Corinthians).

So maybe the problem isn't with Paul's language so much as our lack of a transformed imagination. Maybe the problem is that we still do not see how the cross turns the world's power structures on their heads. Maybe Paul's not insulting the "weak ones"—maybe he's saying they're actually more like Jesus.

Here are Paul's instructions to this divided community. They hold up a mirror to the ways we all too often treat people with whom we differ.

If you're one of "the weak," don't judge. Yes, those people are doing things you think are wrong. MYOB.

If you're one of "the strong," don't despise. Yes, those people are unnecessarily abstaining from something that's okay. MYOB.

---

[1] Priscilla and Aquila are in Ephesus with Paul when he writes 1 Corinthians (see 1 Corinthians 16:19), but he greets them as part of the community in Rome at the end of Romans (Romans 16:3).

And Paul suffuses these instructions with what God has done, is doing and will do. Why not judge? Because God has already accepted the person you want to condemn (Romans 14:3). Because the Lord Jesus will ensure that the person stands and does not fall (14:4).

As humans trying our best to embody our identity as God's children, the thing we must realize is that we each make our choices based on our understanding of how best to serve the Lord (14:5–8). Some decisions look like death, some look like life—and the Dead and Resurrected One is Lord over both (14:9).

But we have an even greater obligation than just keeping our judgy thoughts to ourselves. We live in community. And that community is supposed to be telling the Jesus story with everything it is and does.

"Don't put a stumbling block in a sibling's way" (14:13). When does a decision to eat or not eat become a really big problem? When we give offense to our siblings (14:14). Bread ceases to be merely bread when it trips up our brother or sister (14:20).

The culminating verse of chapter 14 states that choices about food and drink (and festival days and circumcision, we might add) all are a matter of faith. If you have doubts and eat anyway, you are sinning—you are not acting out of faith.

Anything that is not "of faith" is sin (14:23).

Remember that in Romans, the phrase "of faith" does not just refer to what we think, or even our own trust in God. The world "of faith" begins with God's faithfulness to honor God's promises and culminates in Christ's faithfulness in going to the cross.

Seeing God in Your Sibling's Face

The question, then, is not simply what do we think in our hearts. The question is what arises from the story of God's faithfulness to us in the faithfulness of Christ. This is why we are not simply free to eat, full stop. We who are strong must use our strength for the good of our neighbor. We must bear their weakness (15:1–2). We have a positive obligation to serve our siblings.

This is Paul's version of "Do unto others as you would have them do unto you." It's not enough to not do what you don't want them to do. We must empathetically understand where they are, submit ourselves to emotions and desires that are not our own, and please them for their own good (15:2).

Why? Because this is the Jesus story. "Even Christ did not please himself, but as it is written, 'The insults of those who insulted you fell upon me'" (Romans 15:3, quoting Psalm 69:9).

Who is "you" in that verse? In the psalm, it's God. The psalmist is composing a litany of ways he has been wronged by his opponents. His faithfulness to God has led to his being mocked and insulted. "The insults of those who insult you, God, fell on me, your servant."

What happens when we marry this psalm to Paul's letter? Paul says that Jesus takes up this psalm, that it applies to him. In other words, Jesus didn't please himself; instead, he bore the insults of the people who insulted God.

Paul is telling the Romans to be like Jesus: that same Jesus who didn't please himself. He's asking them to play the part of Jesus. He's inviting them to narrate this dynamic of the Jesus story in their life together. This means "bearing the insults" that are hurled at God.

But the crazy part is the application. The way you "bear God's insults" is to bear with your "weaker sibling." This injunction only makes sense once we recognize that the "weaker sibling" is someone who embodies the presence of God. This is sort of like the Gospels, where the smallest child is the stand-in for Jesus and God (Mark 9:36–37). Paul is saying that if you want to be like Jesus, then you need to see that God is present in your "weaker sibling." Bear the insults that might be cast on them. Accept them. Be like Jesus.

In the context of Romans 14–15, these "weaker siblings" were the members of the community who avoided meat and drink in their efforts to keep the law. In other words, they were the Christian Jews.

In a world where Gentiles (i.e., Rome) ruled, this was the strongest possible admonition for Christian Gentiles to love the Jewish people among them as physical embodiments of the presence of God.

What's the end game here? Where does bearing one another's burdens and accepting one another lead? In Paul's vision, to a place where "Together, with one voice, you glorify God" (Romans 15:6).

I feel like that verse could be a Jeopardy answer. "Alex, what is something that churches really haven't cared about for at least the past 500 years?"

Unity. Diverse peoples in the same building lifting one voice to glorify God.

But Paul cares. This whole elaborate letter has been a theological and practical roadmap for overcoming the greatest divide in the history of the church. The only hope is to embody the Jesus story. Accepting as Christ accepted. Laying down our lives for one another as Christ did for us. Pleasing each other as Christ pleased God.

Telling the Jesus Story Together

Paul's final word to the church before delivering his last greetings is this: accept one another. Just like Christ accepted you. (Romans 15:7). In other words, let your church tell the Jesus story.

For the Romans, this story has two prongs. Christ shows the truth and faithfulness of God by first fulfilling the promises to the Jewish ancestors, then by allowing the Gentiles to praise God for God's mercy (15:8–9).

Paul believes that this Jew-plus-Gentile people-of-God scenario fulfills multiple scripture passages. God's name praised among the Gentiles is something only a Jew could accomplish, because only they know the Name. In fulfillment of Psalm 18, a Jew can go out and sing praises to the name of God among the Gentiles—this is what Paul sees happening with the ingathering of the Gentiles through his mission (Romans 15:9, citing Psalm 18:49).

Paul sees Deuteronomy 32:43 being fulfilled through this as well: "Rejoice, Gentiles, *with* God's people" (Romans 15:10). If the gospel of Jesus is going to fulfill the scriptures—if God, indeed, is going to be proved righteous when God is judged (Rom 3:4)—Jews and Gentiles must be together.

And finally, Paul quotes Isaiah 11:10, which reiterates the three core components of the gospel he laid out in the opening of Romans:

1. There will come the root of Jesse (see Romans 1:3—the messiah is a descendant of David),
2. who arises to rule over the Gentiles (this is an allusion to the resurrection of Jesus from the dead; see Romans 1:4—the Messiah is installed as son of God by the resurrection),
3. the Gentiles will hope in him (see Romans 1:5—Paul's mission is to bring the Gentiles into the people).

Here is the paradox of Paul's message and of his mission. Yes, this is Israel's God. Yes, this is the promise to the Jews. However, that promise is to redeem, restore and unite the whole world, including Gentiles.

The resurrection means that the Messiah's throne transcends the geographical and ethnic boundaries into which any nation or people group might attempt to place him. Jesus rules over all. And here "all" means both Jews and Gentiles. All finding joy in their thanksgiving feast. Together. With or without wine.

CHAPTER SIXTEEN

Romans 15:14–16:27: See You Soon

Paul's Purposes

"It's been too long. Let's catch up again soon."—My version of how to end a letter (…okay, an email) to someone I haven't seen in a long time.

"Been too long! Sorry I haven't gotten there yet, but God basically wanted me to preach the gospel to every human who lives east of you before I showed. So there was that. Also, I'm heading back to Jerusalem to fulfill Isaiah's vision of the ingathering of the Gentiles' riches. But I'm going to knock that out, and then I'll see you in a few!"—Paul's version

That's basically the rest of the chapter for you.

Romans 15 describes the intricate interlacing of Paul's travel plans, how Jewish–Gentile unity was manifested in the collection of money for Christian Jews living in Jerusalem, and the role of Rome in the future westward expansion of the gospel message. Along with chapter 16, it provides us some clues about Paul's motivation for writing the letter to the Romans.

As we discussed in the introduction, each of these points offer valid insights into the complex moment in which Paul finds himself. Additionally, the issues of theology and church practice that he hopes will guide the Romans' life together are the same issues that got him into trouble in Galatia, and that are casting a pall over his upcoming trip to Jerusalem.

The final paragraphs of Romans raise some tricky questions, and scholars are still debating which of these are the most important for understanding Paul's missive. For my part, I hold them loosely, allowing them to sit together as indications of a complicated moment in Paul's life and the life of the early church. In light of these questions and their possible answers, Romans might have more than one purpose.

Is Romans a missionary support letter? When he mentions the Roman church helping him on his way to Spain, is Paul finally showing his fund-raising hand (Romans 15:24)?

Or is the letter intended mostly for Gentile Christians in Rome, instructing them to demonstrate appropriate humility toward Christian Jews? And, speaking of his audience, how is it that this particular epistle contains the longest list of greetings out of all of Paul's letters (16:1–16), even though he'd never visited Rome?

Or is this letter written less with Rome in mind, and more as an expression of the hopes and fears, dreams and anxieties that Paul is carrying with him as he prepares to go to Jerusalem, supported by money from the churches in Macedonia and Achaia (15:24–32)?

If you read Galatians and 2 Corinthians, the letters that Paul wrote just before Romans, you get the clear sense that not everyone is happy with his version of the law-free Gentile mission. And Paul anticipates that not everyone in Judea will be happy to see him (15:31).

What Paul Has Done

In the context of "not everyone is happy with Paul," some of what he says in chapter 15 is a bit more understandable. The apostle is defending himself.

> God has given me the gift of being a minister, a priest of this gospel (15:15–16).

The Spirit has made holy my offering to God—which is the Gentiles themselves (15:16).

Christ, through me, made the Gentiles obedient in word and deed (15:18).

The Gentiles are showing that they've received the Spirit's power through signs and wonders (15:19).

This little ol' thing that God gave me to do? Just so ya know, it's nothing less than the fulfillment of Isaiah's prophecy (15:21).

Notice how Paul's own integrity as a person stands or falls on the truth or falsity of his claim that God has accepted the Gentiles into the family of Israel. You see the same thing happening in Acts. Receiving the Spirit is not just about a personal experience of connecting with God. It's proof that God has accepted people who would otherwise be considered outsiders. It's proof that God has moved the boundaries.

Paul isn't just being a boastful egoist. Okay, he might be boasting. But he's not *just* doing that. More importantly, he's making a case for these people. For those who are the fruit of his mission. He is making the case that the people of God now include those who have responded to his message—and that this is all God's doing. Otherwise, God would not be faithful. Otherwise, there would not be a manifestation of the righteousness of God.

Paul is genuinely worried about "the disobedient in Judea" (15:31). Our best guess is that he's referring to the conservative, law-keeping Christian Jews who disagree with how he's refiguring the identity of God's people. They vehemently oppose Paul's arguments that it's possible to serve the God of Israel without clinging to all the Bible's instructions.

Remember all the strange biblical interpretations we saw through Romans? The "disobedient" would be the ones disagreeing with these interpretations. They would be the ones maintaining that nobody can join the people of God without adhering to the traditional standards: keeping Torah, keeping food laws, keeping Sabbath, being circumcised.

Paul knows just how radical it was to claim that a Jew is someone who has been circumcised in the heart (Romans 2:29)—as if heart circumcision is enough, without physical circumcision. He knows that other followers of Jesus—especially Jewish followers of Jesus in Jerusalem—vehemently disagree with him.

The Collection

Scholars speculate that this tension is one of the major driving forces behind a massive fundraising campaign that Paul had undertaken over the previous year or so (15:25–27; see 1 Corinthians 16:1–4 and 2 Corinthians 8–9; yes, that's two whole chapters of 2 Corinthians on the subject). Here, Paul says that the intention is reciprocity: the Gentiles shared in the Jews' spiritual blessings, so they have an obligation to minister out of their material wealth.

Another angle on the collection plate might be Paul's vision of himself as one who is bringing Isaiah's prophecies to fulfillment. In Isaiah 66, for instance, we read of the wealth of the nations and the Gentiles themselves streaming to Jerusalem after word of God's salvation has gone out.

Isaiah promised that the nations would see God's glory. Paul has shown it to them. This offering places a bow on Isaiah's picture of the future.

As we saw in chapter 11, so we see here as well: Paul views himself as standing at the turning of the ages. Yes, he inhabits the years in the immediate aftermath of Jesus's ministry. But more importantly, on a cosmic scale, his mission marks the moment where God's climactic plans for Israel are coming to a head. Indeed, his ministry, supported by the Gentiles' offering, could be the very thing that moves Israel to jealousy and leads to their salvation (Romans 11:14).

For Your Next Quiet Time

You can be forgiven for not meditating on the list of names in Romans 16:1–16 during your quiet time. But there are some gems in there if you know how to look—especially if you're open to seeing how much women were doing in the early church.

Paul first commends Phoebe to the Roman church (16:1–2). She is a deacon. Do you hear that, my Southern Baptist friends, oh church of my youth, oh church that suckled and nurtured me in my infancy? Paul is 100% down with female deacons.

Don't miss Priscilla and Aquila (16:3–4). Good on them for making the Romans list. Interestingly, when Paul writes 1 Corinthians from Ephesus, he includes a greeting from them. Now he's in Corinth, and they have gone to Rome. Some scholars believe that Priscilla and Aquila were displaced to Corinth when Claudius expelled the Jews from Rome, and that they were subsequently allowed to return.

This would explain a lot. Imagine a Gentile church existing in Rome, by itself, and then having to reincorporate its Jewish siblings when they got back home. You'd have to figure out how to accommodate a different set of social practices, theologies and expectations. You might need a letter like Romans to guide you through the relationship.

Andronicus and Junia are another important pair (16:7). The Greek describes them as "outstanding among the apostles" (*epistēmoi en tois apostolois*) though some translations have done their best to obscure this. The implication, of course, is that they are, together, an apostolic couple, and a woman was counted among the number of apostles. That makes her a teacher. That makes her a bearer of authority.

You know how we know that this is probably the right interpretation? Because a long line of manuscript evidence shows us that people changed her name to a masculine form. Uncomfortable with a woman being called an apostle, so they edited the Bible to reflect their beliefs in women's subordination. But it's still there. A female apostle.

The list is actually astounding for its number of women, though we know little of what Paul would mean by calling someone a "laborer in the Lord" (16:12) or what kind of work Persida (definitely a female name, because the adjective "beloved" is in the feminine form) might have done (16:12).

I sometimes have visions of "meet the Bible character day" in heaven. There are Patrobas and Phlegon, playing checkers together, wondering if anyone will ever recognize them. If this happens, please keep an eye out. When you see them, run up, look them in the eye and say, "Romans 16, right?!" I think you'll make their day.

Odd Ends

As a New Testament scholar with a Ph.D. conferred upon me for my work on Romans, I would like to offer a professional opinion. I (not the Lord) say that Romans 16:17–20 is weird. That's a technical term we use in the biblical studies guild.

It's weird in that it interjects a random paragraph of teaching and admonition into the middle of the closing greetings (that's not usually how letters were written in the ancient world). It's weird because the way it talks about opponents and false teachers is out of step with the rhetoric of the rest of the letter. Up until now, the "opponent" Paul has addressed has been rhetorical. He has used hypothetical questions and disagreements to propel his argument. He has spoken of real-life issues and challenges around the identity of the people of God and how people should live. But he has not spoken of real-life opponents who disagree with his teaching.

Paul only mentions "Satan" in the letter once (right here in 16:20). Of course, Paul does mention Satan in other writings (e.g., 1 Corinthians 5:5, 7:5; 2 Corinthians 2:11), but in Romans, the everyday spiritual opponents have more often been "the flesh," "sin" and "death."

But then, there's something delightfully paradoxical in saying that the God of peace will soon crush Satan underneath your feet. Ah ... the ol' peace-through-stomping-Satan trick. Nice. Just as long as we don't identify human beings as Satanic emissaries deserving such a fate. That's where things go sideways.

So what do we make of this "weird" paragraph? A lot of New Testament scholars believe that it was a later addition to the letter.

Prior to the printing press, every piece of writing that was distributed had to be copied by hand. Material sometimes was added according to the needs of the day—or according to the proclivities of the scribe making the copy.

It is hard to say for sure in this case. I would just recommend holding this "weird" paragraph with open hands. Read it, interpret it, and apply it in light of the larger Christ-story. The story of self-giving love. The story that calls us to refrain from taking our own revenge. The story that gives us a vision of the reconciliation of the entire cosmos.

As he often does, Paul sends final greetings prior to giving a last blessing (16:21–24). You'll probably recognize Timothy. Sosipater's got winner of the Patrobas v. Phlegon checkers game.

And then there's the big reveal. Paul didn't write Romans! Tertius did (16:22)!

Okay, so Paul did write it. And so did Tertius. It was common practice for a scribe to write a letter as it was either dictated or outlined by someone else. The amount of freedom said scribe had varied. But to an extent that we can't ever know for sure, Tertius had a hand in writing Romans.

Final Farewell, with a Flourish

The letter ends with a blessing that recapitulates several of its larger themes (16:25–27). There is power in the gospel Paul proclaims. The gospel itself is the manifestation of the mystery: God's promise that finds fulfillment in unexpected ways.

The mystery was hidden in scripture, which has now been fulfilled; and with that fulfillment, the mystery is disclosed. It's not kept secret anymore but is openly proclaimed (v. 26). What does it mean that something is "hidden" in scripture? Maybe this is Paul's way of describing how he reads the Bible. All that strange interpretation is, in fact, disclosing through biblical readings what God has disclosed in Jesus.

And the result? "The obedience of faith." This is the same phrase Paul used in Romans 1:5 to discuss his Gentile mission. And thus, the letter receives its bookend.

God's purpose, the fulfillment of scripture, Jesus as Messiah, Paul as emissary—all these things have a singular purpose. That purpose is the obedience of faith, overflowing the bounds of Israel and embracing the nations.

This is the wisdom of God, for which Paul calls everyone to render praise and glory. "To the only wise God, through Jesus Christ, be glory forever. Amen."

GUIDE

FOR GROUP DISCUSSIONS

How to Use this Guide

Books are better when they're shared, and this is especially true when we're talking about the Bible. Don't believe us? Just ask the ancient Israelites, early Christians and oh, just about everyone who lived before the invention of the printing press.

But it can be hard to stay on track, particularly when you're engaging in a group discussion, so we've created this chapter-by-chapter guide to help you as you dive into the book of Romans—together.

This guide includes:

- *A Summary* of each chapter.
- *Discussion Questions* to help spark conversation. (Some are open-ended, while others require you to do some digging in the biblical text.)
- *Big Conversations with Little Ones* questions to inspire big conversations with the little ones in your life.
- *Notes for Leaders* to help leaders prepare and lead the group in conversation. (To fill in more information where needed, we also recommend using a good study Bible, such as *The Jewish Study Bible*, *The Harper Collins Study Bible*, *The New Oxford Annotated Bible*, or *The New Interpreter's Study Bible*.)

So let's get started …

1. Romans from 30,000 Feet

Summary

Romans isn't about predestination. It's not systematic theology. And it's not about thinking the right things.

Romans is about the family of God. Who they are, where they've come from and—most importantly—how they live. Right here, right now. A family recreated through the resurrection of Jesus Christ. A family that so bears the likeness of God, observers can look at them and know exactly who God is.

Throughout Romans, Paul draws heavily on the Hebrew scriptures, re-interpreting them through the lens of his lived experience in a post-resurrection world. A world in which the Jewish people—Paul's people!—have largely not accepted Jesus as Messiah, while countless Gentiles have adopted this story as their own.

As such, Romans has much wisdom to offer us. Wisdom about how to live in community with those with whom we disagree. How to live lives of self-sacrifice in service to our neighbors. How to trust in the faithfulness of God. And how to trust that God's name receives greater praise from a motley group of worshippers than a monolithic group of people just like us.

Discussion Questions

1. How has your understanding of Paul's message(s) in Romans changed or evolved over time?
2. What influences have helped shape your understanding?
3. How might Paul's re-interpretation of the Hebrew Bible inform your own approach to reading Paul's letter to the Romans today?

   Note for Leaders: Episode 45: Romans for Normal People of the Bible for Normal People podcast canvasses 10 things to be aware of when you read Romans. It provides a good jumping off point for initial study group discussions.

Big Conversations with Little Ones

1. What do you think God wants you to know more than anything else in the world?
2. How do you know this?
3. What are some words you would use to describe God? How does God show you this is who God is?

2. Romans 1:1–17: Introducing Romans

Summary

Right from the get-go, Paul establishes the deep scriptural and historical roots of his message and reiterates the unexpected way in which Jesus's promised power and enthronement come about—through his resurrection. For Paul, the resurrection of Jesus established the new age—the new creation itself.

Jesus in Romans is the entrée for the rest of us into the new-creation family of God. And it all starts with trust: Jesus entrusts himself to God, even to the point of death. The death and resurrection of Jesus are where the faithfulness of humanity and the righteousness of God meet. God does what is right by giving resurrection life and an eternal kingdom to the Messiah who was faithful to the point of death.

As Paul tells it, the story of God is the story of the Jewish scriptures, which is the story of Jesus, which is the story of us. Romans is an extended dance on this web of interconnection, in which Paul's present determines his reading of the past.

For God to be righteous, a certain kind of people must be formed. A people consisting of Jew and Gentile. A people who demonstrate through their faithful obedience the transformative power of God's life-giving Spirit. This is why Romans had to be written: it's the people. They're off kilter. And it's calling into question whether God is, in fact, as righteous as Paul claims.

Discussion Questions

1. How does understanding the resurrection as the moment in which Jesus assumed God's sonship interact with your understanding of Jesus as God's son? And with other biblical accounts of Jesus?
   Note for Leaders: *Contrast Paul's understanding with the accounts of Jesus's birth in Luke 1:26–35, baptism in Mark 1:9–11, and eternal being in John 1:1–18.*

2. In many ways, our own relationship with Paul is similar to that of many in the Roman church, as we know him only through the words he wrote. What are your impressions of Paul and his legacy? Have these changed over time?

3. How does the interdependence between God's righteousness and the formation of a particular kind of people interact with your understanding of God?

4. Using this framework and looking at the church today, how would you rate God's righteousness? Why?

Big Conversations with Little Ones

1. Who is Jesus? How do you know this?
2. Who gets to be part of God's family?
3. How do you think God would like his family to act (or behave)? Towards God? Towards each other? Towards themselves?

3. Romans 1:18–2:29: We're in This Together

Summary

In the latter half of Romans 1, Paul steps fully into an assumed Jewish identity and talks about the failures of the Gentiles: the ones who rejected the revelation of God. To do this, he trots out a decline of civilization framework: namely, an anti-creation narrative with allusions to Genesis 1.

Paul tells this anti-creation narrative not to shame the Gentiles, but rather to show his own people—the Jews—that they best not judge anyone before they take a long, hard look at themselves.

Romans 1:18–2:29 not only levels the playing field by proclaiming that Gentiles and Jews are equally guilty—equally in need of God's mercy and equally requiring transforming power to live as God desires—it also radically redefines what it means to be the people of God ... which is to say, what it means to be Jewish.

Paul does this through a bold rhetorical move that's more challenging and dangerous than rejecting Judaism's house rules. He doesn't deny that keeping God's commandments or being circumcised are critical to the identity of the people of God. Instead, he reinterprets what these beloved, God-given symbols mean: circumcision becomes the work of the Spirit, while law-keeping becomes the obedience of faith. The external markers of the Jewish people are Spiritualized and, therefore, accessible to everyone.

Discussion Questions

1. If Paul were writing Romans today, what behaviors or characteristics might he populate his anti-creation narrative with?

2. Where are the "us" and "them" boundaries in your own life and
    in the life of your faith community? How are these upheld?
    Where is there unity?
    Note for Leaders: *This could easily become a discussion devoted*
    to the boundaries in the community's life; gently push back on this.
    Though these are important to name and acknowledge, they should
    not be used to avoid interrogating personal us/them boundaries.
3. Can you think of an example of a community that does unity
    well? What does "well" mean to you and what did it look like
    in practice?

Big Conversations with Little Ones

1. Has anyone ever made you feel like you didn't belong, or like
    they weren't your friend? How did that make you feel?
2. How do you think that made God feel?
3. How do you think God wants us to make each other feel?

4. Romans 3: The Faith of God

Summary

How can God still be considered faithful if God's work of salvation is
leaving the Jewish people behind?

Paul begins by asking whether Jewish "faithlessness" will nullify
God's "faithfulness?" Of course not, says Paul. God will be faithful.
God will stand by what God has spoken and will be justified by God's
own words. God is justified because God kept faith with Israel.

However, Paul's claim comes at a price: he creates a gap between
God and the people of Israel. Worse, he ties God's justification to the
people's failure.

Paul turns God's gift of the law on the people of the law, claiming it doesn't make the Jewish people the faithful people of God. Rather, the law illuminates the full extent of their need for forgiveness. It's not that the law itself is bad, it's just that Jesus changed everything.

Paul urges his fellow Jews to view the law through the lens of Jesus and his faithfulness in dying on the cross, and to see this as an act of faithfulness that also justifies God. Because through the resurrection of Jesus, God is doing the right thing in relationship to Israel, i.e. doing what God promised to do in scripture. It's a cosmic answer to the primal promise. God's justification by faith, no less than our own, hinges on the death of Jesus.

Paul wants the Jesus story to become this rag-tag collection of believers' founding story, their hermeneutic and their way of life. The story that binds together a new people. That is what it means to be justified by God's faith.

Discussion Questions

1. Paul wrestles deeply with the goodness of God, performing intricate theological contortions to prove God's faithfulness. How do you reconcile the goodness of God with those things in the world that cause you to question it?
2. How does this influence your engagement with God and with the world?
3. How has your understanding of justification by faith evolved over time? Who (or what) has influenced your understanding?

Big Conversations with Little Ones

1. Can you think of a time someone acted in a way that made you wonder whether they really did believe the things they said they did?

Big people: *If needed, provide examples such as, someone cheating in a card game when they say it's important to be honest or saying something mean when they say it's important to be kind.*

2. Have you ever acted in a way that wasn't consistent with (the same as) your beliefs? Why did you do this?
3. What kind of person do you think God created you to be? How do your actions show that?

5. Romans 4: Father Abraham?

Summary

In Romans 4, Paul sets about reworking the idea of Abraham as forefather. Along the way, he reconstructs the identity of Abraham's God so that it meshes perfectly with the gospel message Paul proclaims.

Paul begins by asking whether Abraham is our forefather according to the flesh. The implied answer to this rhetorical question is "no," because Abraham is our forefather according to faith. In verses 1–15, Paul argues that Abraham's justification comes prior to the outward sign of his faith: circumcision. Therefore, Abraham is forefather of those with faith, circumcised or not.

This was an extraordinary—unbelievable even—claim for ancient Jews. Indeed, Paul could only make it by viewing Abraham through the lens of Jesus. We all do this: read scripture through the lens of our own experiences in the world.

Paul spends verses 16–25 emphasizing the resurrection god of Jesus is the same resurrection god of Abraham, who brought forth life from Abraham's ancient (already dead) body and Sarah's barren (dead) womb. Abraham believed what Paul proclaims: God is the one who raises the dead.

For the people of God to take on a new identity, God's identity must be understood in a fresh way as well.

Discussion Questions

1. Paul quotes Genesis 15.6 in Romans 4:3 (and Gal. 3.6) to argue Abraham was justified by his faith, yet James 2:23 uses this same passage to argue Abraham was justified by faith and works (referring to the binding of Isaac, Genesis 22). What do you make of a Bible that retains two opposing interpretations of the same story?

2. How does your understanding of justification by faith interact with your understanding of justification by works?
   Note for Leaders: *The following passages may provide a jumping off point for discussion: Micah 6:8, Matthew 25:31–46, James 2:14–18, 1 John 3:18.*

3. Paul argues Abraham's faith did not weaken (Rom 4:19) when he considered the barrenness of Sarah's womb. Reflecting on Genesis 16, would you agree with Paul's assessment or not? Why or why not? If you disagree, does this change how you might view Paul's reading of other Old Testament passages and stories?

Big Conversations with Little Ones

1. What do you find surprising about God?
2. Which Bible stories do you find surprising?
3. Have you ever heard someone talk about a story in the Bible and thought, "huh...I feel differently about that"? What was the story and how did you think differently about it?

6. Romans 5: Stitching a Story, Beginning to End

Summary

In the first half of Romans 5, Paul connects the dots between the past and the future in a way that has the power to radically transform the present into a place of peace, because of where the story came from and where it's going.

What is the future that Paul sees? "The glory of God." Not just that we "glorify God," but that we are the glory of God. But if we are going to reflect the fullness of God's glory, we need to get the fullness of God's people into the room.

In the second part of Romans 5, Paul takes a slightly convoluted wander back to where it all began: Adam. Sin. And sin's power.

Adam's transgression unleashed a reign of terror. Adam's actions had consequences for all of humanity: sin's power enslaved humanity and brought with it death.

Enter: Jesus. The freedom to Adam's enslavement, the victory to Adam's failure. So, where Adam's action brought death, we would expect Jesus's action to bring…well…life. Instead, the people who accept God's gift of grace, in Christ, will reign in life.

Jesus's actions restore humanity to its pre-Adam vocation—God's intent for God's image bearers—as rulers over God's creation. Rulers like the God of Genesis 1: life-giving, empowering, generous. Rulers like the God who regains power through self-sacrifice at the cross. Rulers like the God whose grace increased as sin did.

Discussion Questions

1. Paul draws heavily on the Genesis account of Adam to explain how sin's power took hold of humanity. Read

Genesis 2:15–3:24: how does your reading of this story (and its consequences) compare with Paul's?

Note for leaders: Chapter 4 of Genesis for Normal People provides an overview of the significance (and symbolism) of Adam's story for ancient Israelites. This additional context provides rich content for further discussions on this topic.

2. How does your reading of Genesis 2 and 3 interact with your understanding of Jesus's death on the cross (if at all)?

3. How would you compare humanity's rule over creation with that of God's rule in Genesis 1? How do the actions of your (faith) community compare with the characteristics of God's rule in Genesis 1?

Big Conversations with Little Ones

1. Why do you think the world needed Jesus?
2. Why do you think we sometimes do things that hurt God and each other?
3. Why do you think God created people?

7. Romans 6: Jesus: Where We Live and Move and Have Our Being

Summary

Should we continue in sin in order that grace may abound? No way, says Paul. In fact, this question misses the point of the whole story. We are to embody a different moment—the story's saving moment. We enter the story at the point of deliverance.

And how do we enter this story? The Spirit is important, as is the Lord's Supper. But according to Paul, baptism is the most crucial step to being "in Christ." And when we take on Jesus's identity, the things that are true about him become true of us, as well.

Here's the often-overlooked part of being in union with Christ: it's not just about becoming a different kind of person—a "Christ person," if you will; it is also about the formation of a new people. Together. A new humanity for the new creation God is bringing about.

We share the Jesus narrative. This is where the idea that sin and death are powers that would rule over humanity comes to the fore. As powers, they imposed a rule and a way of life. Jesus, through his death and resurrection, went through that rule and came out the other side to the rule of God and life and grace. Now we get to—need to—have Jesus's narrative become our own narrative as well. We are a people "alive from the dead."

And those who aren't "in Christ?" Well, Paul's belief is they will die. No hell. No eternal condemnation. Judgement? Yes. But the consequences are death. Simply ceasing to exist. So Paul offers his readers a choice: slavery to sin (and death) or slavery to obedience which leads to righteousness (and life).

Discussion Questions

1. How does Paul's understanding of baptism compare with your own understanding of how one comes to be "in Christ?" How does this compare with the theology and practices of your faith community?

2. Does your understanding of what comes after death mirror or differ from Paul's?
   Note for Leaders: The following passages provide a glimpse of the diversity of views in the Bible: Psalm 6:5, Psalm 115:17, Psalm 146: 4, Ecclesiastes 9:5–10, Daniel 12:1–3, Matthew 25:31–46, John 14:1–4, Revelation 21:8.

For a deeper dive, check out episodes 21 (Resurrection in the Hebrew Bible), 118 (Does Hell Exist?) and 149 (The End Times and American Christian Culture) of the Bible for Normal People podcast, or head over to theb4np on TikTok and watch #53 Is Hell Real?

3. "Theological diversity is an inherent part of Christianity: a feature rather than a bug." Do you see this statement reflected in the life of your community? How do you engage with those holding differing theological views?

Big Conversations with Little Ones

1. How do people become part of God's family?
2. How does your family or church mark special times in the lives of the people in your community?
    Big people: *You might think about things like baptism, communion, weddings, funerals, graduations, birthdays etc.*
3. What does loving Jesus look like in your family?

8. Romans 7: Legal Troubles

Summary

Romans 7 unfolds in three parts. First, Paul uses the analogy of marriage to show the limits of the law: a widow is no longer bound by law to her husband after death, just as Jews are no longer bound to the law after death ... and resurrection. Throughout his analogy, Paul aligns the law with death and sin.

Then, the about face: does this mean the law is sin? No! But sin took hold of it like a weapon and that's how you know how bad sin is: it can take something good and use it for terrible purposes. Throughout Paul's letters he is rewriting the story, struggling to give the law its proper place. Something holy, righteous and good in itself (Romans 7:12), and yet implicated in the reign of sin and death.

Paul concludes with some of his most instantly recognizable words: "The things I do, I don't understand, because I don't do the things that I wish to do, but the things I don't wish to do? Yeah, I do those." (7:15–19; paraphrased, obviously.) Though this passage has resonated with Christians down through the centuries as a picture of their own life struggles, that is likely not what Paul is trying to portray. Paul seems to be assuming the voice of a character and is probably speaking of the life of Israel outside of Christ. His words describe the very conflict that being in Christ should fully resolve.

Discussion Questions

1. Of the laws you have lived under, which are non-negotiable for you? How would you react if a foreign visitor mocked or broke the laws you most value?
2. Compare Paul's statement in Romans 7:9 with Deuteronomy 30:15–16. How do these views of the law differ theologically? Which (if either) of these theological positions resonates most strongly with you? Which do you see reflected in the life of your faith community?
3. What is your response to reading Romans 7:15–19 as a character representing a conflict that being in Christ should fully resolve?

Big Conversations with Little Ones

1. What are some of your family rules?
2. Which ones are you glad you have? Which would you change if you could?
3. How would you feel if your friend came over to your house and broke one of your family rules? What would you do?

9. Romans 8: Resurrection People

Summary

Romans 8 is a description of the all-encompassing transformation made possible through the Spirit who raised Jesus from the dead. Being "in the Spirit" while still inhabiting a fleshy body means we no longer inhabit the realm where the flesh is subjected to sin and death; we are in the realm where the Spirit and life and righteousness hold sway. Just as Jesus "becomes" God's son when he is raised and enthroned as Spirit-transformed Lord, we become God's children through the Spirit that confers Jesus's sonship on us.

When Paul looks to the future it is not to imagine humans floating off to heaven to be with God in the sky forever. The biblical narrative can only be concluded where it started: with all of creation rightly ordered, flourishing, thriving, being fruitful and multiplying, as God originally intended. And with a faithful humanity embodying the truth of God's own presence upon its land.

Paul hopes that even as Jesus's move from suffering to glory sets us free, so too our move from suffering to glory will set all of creation free. This is what people have been "set aside" for: this is the Purpose. The purpose of being restored to the fullness of what it means to be truly human. Which is to say, to be transformed into the image of Jesus.

What is the source of hope? God. With God as the insurance for glory in the age to come, and with Jesus as our own embodied future at God's right hand, the future is not in doubt. All potential enemies are mocked. The love of Christ, the love of God, triumphs in the end.

Discussion Questions

1. Many verses in Romans 8 are in themselves transformative for many Christians. Which (if any) holds special meaning for you? How has it impacted your life of faith?

2. How does the idea of a restored creation interact with your understanding of what is to come? How does it interact with your faith tradition's beliefs or teachings on this subject?

3. Read Romans 8:35–39. Do you share Paul's confidence? Why or why not?

Big Conversations with Little Ones

1. Why do you think God gave us bodies?
2. What would your community look like if everyone acted like Jesus?
3. Describe how you imagine the world would be if God's dreams for it came true.

10. So, About the Cross

Summary

For better or worse, Paul's understanding of the cross is that the death and resurrection of Jesus are what God has orchestrated to bring salvation, forgiveness, justification and resurrection life. This means for every one of the world's problems (think "sin" and "death") the death and resurrection of Jesus are the solution. And God is the one who choreographed it.

Did it have to happen? Paul thinks so.

In contrast, a trinitarian lens allows us to view the cross not as an act of divine child-sacrifice, but a powerful act of self-sacrifice.

Is this what happened? Many think so.

Wherever you land, both Paul's reinterpretation of Jewish scriptures through the lens of the cross and the trinitarian approach (which is entirely foreign to scripture) provide models of biblical interpretation we can follow to engage with and interpret the scriptures in our own place and time, acknowledging that our experiences of God and our knowledge of the world shape and influence our theologies. In doing this, we can faithfully continue this Jesus story, which did not end in the first century. This is, really, the only way we can be "biblical."

Discussion Questions

1. How do you understand the cross?
2. How does your understanding of the cross influence or reflect your understanding of God's character?
3. How does your understanding of God's character influence your lived faith (your actions in the world)?

Big Conversations with Little Ones

1. Can you think of a story in the Bible where someone was saved? What were they saved from? Who saved them? What did being saved look like?
   Big people: if your little ones can't recall any specific stories, you could suggest Moses being saved by the midwives, the Israelites being saved from Egypt's Pharaoh or Daniel from the lions.
2. Why did Jesus die?
3. Why does God let bad things happen?

11. Romans 9: Mystery and Yearning

Summary

Romans 9 is the heart-rending cry for loved ones left behind. It's all been heading to this point where Paul grapples with the harsh reality that God's chosen people have not chosen Jesus in return. What could this mean for the Jewish people?

Paul reminds his readers that it is God who does the choosing. Isaac, not Ishmael; Jacob, not Esau; Israel, not Pharoah. Not because of anything the chosen or not-chosen had done, but just so God could be the one to choose.

For Paul, the chosen and not-chosen are two sides of the one coin: one cannot exist without the other. Where there is rejection, it is for the sake of salvation. For the Gentiles to be saved, God's son, Israel, is given up.

Discussion Questions

1. Reflect on Paul's examples of the chosen and not-chosen from scripture. Do you agree with Paul when he says, "Is there injustice on God's part? By no means!"
2. How does this chosen and not-chosen interdependence interact with your understanding of salvation?
3. What do you think Paul held true about the character of God? How do these truths compare with your own?

Big Conversations with Little Ones

1. What does it mean to be fair?
2. Does God have to be fair?
3. Is there ever a time it would be wrong to be fair?

12. Romans 10: Rejecting the Gift

Summary

Chapter 10 expresses Paul's heartfelt longing for Israel to come to faith in Jesus. His desire is "for salvation," and this is where he lays out exactly where Israel stumbled: they were trying to do exactly what the Bible told them God wanted them to do.

The Jews were looking to the law to show them how to act, to establish their righteousness as a people and as persons. In contrast, Paul insists that God's righteousness through Christ is what ultimately saves us. For Paul the fundamental issue is that his fellow Jews are reading and obeying scripture as if Jesus isn't the Messiah.

But all is not lost. Paul believes that the massive influx of Gentiles will make the Jews jealous, prompting them to follow the Gentiles into the fold.

Discussion Questions

1. Read Deuteronomy 30:12–13. How do you feel about Paul's application of this verse in Romans 10:6–8?
2. Paul quoted verses describing the return of exiled Israel in Isaiah 52 but applied them to Gentiles (Rom 10:14–15). Are these verses in Isaiah about the Israelites of Isaiah's day or the Gentiles of Paul's?
3. How does your answer to the above question reflect your understanding of how the Bible works?

Big Conversations with Little Ones

1. Is it more important to think the right things or to do the right things?
2. How do you know what the right things are?
3. Which do you think is most important for God?

13. Romans 11: What Hope Remains for Israel?

Summary

The Jesus story helps Paul interpret not only Israel's past, in its scriptures, but its present and its hope. Theirs is a Christ-hope. Paul hopes for Israel as Abraham hoped for Isaac: hope for life from the hand of the God who gives life to the dead.

Some may have fallen away: branches were broken off. And Gentiles slipped in: branches grafted into the spots left behind. This is the peculiar necessity that Paul sees at work. For some mysterious reason, the Israelite branches needed to be removed in order to allow in the Gentile branches. For Paul, it is a heart-wrenching necessity—one he reiterates over and over. They were disobedient so that you could be obedient; you have been shown mercy so that they can be shown mercy.

Paul longs to see all Israel grafted back on the stalk, which is theirs by rights. He holds onto God as the one who is faithful and righteous by naming the mystery of Israel's circumstance as an embodiment of the Jesus-story: rejected and "dead" as instruments of salvation, hoping to rise again and experience the love of God in Christ.

God is not finished with Israel.

Discussion Questions

1. Do you agree or disagree with Paul's understanding of Israel's "rejection" of Jesus as a means of salvation for Gentiles? Why?
2. Supersessionism is a theology that holds the new covenant made through Jesus superseded (or replaced) the Mosaic covenant, and the Christian church has superseded the Jewish people as God's "true Israel" through this new covenant. How does Romans 11 endorse or dismantle supersessionist theologies?

> ***Note for Leaders:*** *Amy-Jill Levine's 2022 article "Supersessionism: Admit and Address Rather than Debate or Deny" (Religion, Vol 13, No. 2) canvasses some of practical, theological and exegetical issues arising from supersessionist theologies, and provides rich content for further discussions on this topic.*

3. Would you describe your faith community's theologies as supersessionist? How do these theologies manifest themselves practically in the life of your community?

Big Conversations with Little Ones

1. Think of a time you were left out or excluded. How did you feel?
2. Do you think God would exclude someone?
3. Can someone exclude themselves from God? What would God do if this happened?

14. Romans 12–13: Living the Jesus Story: From Death to Resurrection

Summary

Therefore.

Paul has taken this motley bunch of believers on a journey, reminding them where their story started and the significant moments along the way, trying to make sense of that which cannot be explained, and pointing ahead to where it might be going. Now, he describes what it looks like: right here, right now.

Romans 12–15 provides Paul's blueprint for the cultural characteristics he envisages for the church. He describes a people shaped by the cross: discerning, humble, loving, empathetic, self-sacrificial and radically peace-making. Subject to governing authorities. Embodying the fullness of the law. Loving their neighbors as themselves: as individuals and as a community.

Discussion Questions

1. What are your gifts? How do you use these to love others well? Note for Leaders: Some questions to help people struggling with this question include: What brings you joy? Where is the "life" in your day/week/month? What are you good at? What engages your mind/body/heart?
2. Is democracy biblical? Why or why not?
3. When have you struggled with being subject to the governing authorities? How would you view these struggles (and your actions, if any) through the lens of Romans 13:1–7?

Big Conversations with Little Ones

1. What do you love to do?
2. What are some things you are really good at?
3. How can you use these gifts you have to love God and others well?

15. Romans 14:1–15:13: One Body. Really.

Summary

Romans 14:1–15:13 is a guide for Jews and Gentiles living together and serving Jesus together, in life and in death. This is the how-do-we-navigate-the-religious-and-behavioral-differences-among-us guidebook. Should we keep the sabbath ... or not? Should we eat unclean food ... or not?

Yes. To all of it.

Because the kingdom of God is not in food and drink, but in righteousness and peace and joy in the Holy Spirit. If one person thinks it is wrong to eat unclean food, then it is wrong. If another thinks no food is unclean, then no food is unclean. What matters is that the one does not judge the other. Because God has already accepted that person. Because the Lord Jesus will ensure that the person stands and does not fall. These minor quibbles only become issues when we give offense to our siblings because we have made our beliefs about them into a religion, instead of striving for unity in Christ.

For Paul, unity is not found in conformity. Rather, it is found in deep and loving respect for our other—those with whom we disagree. Because only when the community is unified—together, with one voice—can we glorify God.

Discussion Questions

1. In what ways does Paul's understanding of unity challenge you? Are there any ideals or beliefs you believe are more important than unity in Christ?

2. How diverse is your faith community? And how diverse are those with whom you are in relationship with?
   Note for leaders: Prompt participants to consider this question through the lenses of politics, socio-economic background, ethnicity, gender, nationality, and even faith/religion.

3. What are the Jew/Gentile divisions in your community? How are these navigated? Do you think Paul would approve of the way these are handled?

Big Conversations with Little Ones

1. In what ways are you and your friends different?
2. Do those differences matter? If so, what do you do about them?
3. Why do you think God made us all so different from each other?

16. Romans 15:14–16:27: See You Soon

Summary

Romans 15 describes the intricate interlacing of Paul's travel plans, how Jewish–Gentile unity was manifested in the collection of money for Christian Jews living in Jerusalem, and the role of Rome in the future westward expansion of the gospel message.

Not everyone was happy about Paul's mission (see Galatians and 2 Corinthians), which may in part explain the collection he has gathered from Gentile churches and intends to deliver to the (largely Jewish) church in Jerusalem. Paul has a grand view of his work, viewing it as the place where God's climactic plans for Israel are coming to a head: perhaps he believed this offering would move Israel to jealousy and, ultimately, lead to their salvation.

In his final greetings, Paul makes mention of many church leaders and deacons, among them a number of women. And Satan ... though this out-of-character reference is likely a later addition.

And finally—finally!—Paul concludes by reiterating what it's all about. God's purpose, the fulfilment of scripture, Jesus as Messiah and Paul as emissary: obedience of faith. Overflowing the bounds of Israel and embracing the nations.

Discussion Questions

1. What do the names in Paul's final greetings tell you about the church Paul was writing to? In what ways is it similar or different from your own community?
2. How have your feelings about Paul and/or Romans evolved or changed over the course of reading this book?
3. What is one learning you will take from your reading of this book? How might you apply this learning practically in your day-to-day life, and in your interactions with others?

Big Conversations with Little Ones

1. What is one thing you can do this week to love someone like Jesus would love them?
2. What is one thing you and your family could do this week to love someone like Jesus?
3. What is one thing you and your family could do every week to love someone like Jesus?

Things for Normal People to Read or Listen to (Or Not ... No Judgment)

Dunn, James D. G. *The New Perspective on Paul.* 2d rev ed. Grand Rapids: Eerdmans, 2007.

Hays, Richard B. *Echoes of Scripture in the Letters of Paul.* New Haven: Yale University Press, 1993.

—. *The Faith of Jesus Christ: The Narrative Substructure of Galatians 3:1–4:11.* Grand Rapids: Eerdmans, 2002.

—. *Conversion of the Imagination: Paul as Interpreter of Israel's Scripture.* Grand Rapids: Eerdmans, 2005.

Gorman, Michael J. *Romans: A Theological and Pastoral Commentary.* Grand Rapids: Eerdmans, 2022.

Kirk, J. R. Daniel. *Unlocking Romans: Resurrection and the Justification of God.* Grand Rapids: Eerdmans, 2008.

Sanders, E. P. *Paul and Palestinian Judaism.* Minneapolis: Fortress, 1977.

Stowers, Stanley K. *A Rereading of Romans: Justice, Jews, and Gentiles.* Rev. ed. New Haven: Yale University Press, 1997.

Acknowledgements

Be careful when you make decisions. You never know which ones will shape you for the rest of your life. For instance, I decided to accept a bribe from a seminary professor: memorize Romans (in English) and I'd get an A for a 1-credit class. I love A's. Done. And so, Romans has become a constant dialogue partner, and Paul's rhythms and phrasings, no less than his ideas, have worked their way deep into my mind. Thanks for the A, Vern.

Then there was the time I decided that, since Richard Hays was going to be my adviser in grad school and I didn't want to embarrass myself, I should read his book, *The Moral Vision of the New Testament*. No person or book has more profoundly shaped my understanding of what it looks like to faithfully follow Jesus. *Romans for Normal People* is suffused with secondhand wisdom that I learned from Hays. On a personal note, I am filled with gratitude for his unrelenting kindness and support for the past two decades.

If you made it through this book, you've probably noticed that I have had a bit of a theological journey. That's one way to find out who your friends are. I am grateful for the persistent encouragement and friendship of my former teachers, Pete Enns and Steve Taylor, through all my twists and turns. I'm particularly grateful to Pete and to Jared Byas for inviting me to add this contribution to their burgeoning Bible for Normal People empire.

About this Book

About the Author

Daniel Kirk (Ph.D., Duke University) is an award-winning New Testament scholar and author who spent years engaging "normal people" about Bible nerd things through blogs, podcasts, books, and speaking. He currently lives in Dallas, TX and is training to be a physician assistant.

Behind the Scenes

Cover Design Tessa McKay Stultz
Editor Emily Moberg Robinson, Woodshed Editors
Special thanks to the eagle-eyed members of our Patreon community who read through the final draft of the manuscript and provided feedback, caught spelling errors and generally ensured we don't look like fools: Kim Bakaev, Aaron W. Kates, Dorsey Marshall, Dan Scott, Ryan Williams, Mary Wolf and Amy Wood. We couldn't do what we do without you.

Enjoy this Book?

To continue the conversation, head over to thebiblefornormalpeople. com where you can:

- Listen to the only God-ordained podcasts on the internet: The Bible for Normal People and Faith for Normal People
- Join our community for members-only content and perks, and journey alongside others who are asking the tough questions.
- Read hundreds of articles from biblical scholars, theologians and practitioners.
- Buy even more books and exclusive B4NP merch.
- Enrol in one of our online courses and deep dive into your area of interest.

Or follow us on Facebook and Instagram (@thebiblefornormalpeople) for more Bible for Normal People content.

Made in the USA
Columbia, SC
20 January 2023

10755464R00121